MW01232935

Climbers chopping steps up Huntington Ravine's classic ODELL'S GULLY in 1962.
Seven years later the technical revolution that was to change the course of modern ice
climbing began on neighboring PINNACLE GULLY.

Photo by Henry Kendall

An Ice Climber's Guide

To Northern New England

2nd Edition

by **Rick Wilcox**

Edited by S. Peter Lewis

Published by
Huntington Graphics
Burlington, Vermont 05402

Published by **Huntington Graphics**
Burlington, Vermont 05402

ISBN 1-886064-10-5
Second edition, third printing.

Cliff Photographs: David Stone, unless otherwise noted
Action photographs: as credited
Maps and diagrams: Bruce Luetters, S. Peter Lewis
Layout, design and production: S. Peter Lewis
Research: Rick Wilcox, S. Peter Lewis
Editing: S. Peter Lewis
Typesetting: S. Peter Lewis, International Mountain Equipment, Inc.
Printed in Canada
Front cover: Dave Karl on MINDBENDER, Lake Willoughby, VT.,
photo by Ted Hammond
Back cover: John Tremblay ropeless on DRACULA,
Frankenstein Cliff, NH.,
photo by S. Peter Lewis

DISCLAIMER

Ice climbing is an inherently dangerous activity. Both subjective and objective dangers are a part of every climb. This guide is not an instruction manual and purchase or use of it does not guarantee safety or competence. Though great care was taken to insure that the information in this guide is as accurate as possible, errors will undoubtedly be found, some that could potentially affect safety. A big part of safe climbing involves judgement skills, and that doesn't just mean deciding whether a tool placement is good enough to go on. It may also mean deciding to go left when the guidebook says to go right. Guidebooks cannot take the place of experience. There are many avenues to learn safe climbing technique, and quality instruction is highly recommended before venturing onto the ice. The author and publisher of this guidebook can in no way be held responsible or liable for any accidents or injuries resulting from ice climbing.

P R E F A C E

to the

S E C O N D   E D I T I O N

Ice climbing has come a long way since the step-cutting era that ended less than three decades ago. Once regarded as a death defying sport only fit for the certifiably "nuts", ice climbing has matured to the point of near respectabliity.

Adventure has become the great ambition of today's generation. In a world of accelerating intensity, the stress of every day life seems to almost require an equally stressful release. It's often not enough to spend liesure time on the golf course or ski slope. Release is found today by being on that half-terrifying, half-thrilling edge found in the middle of a class V whitewater drop, or in those fleeting moments before the bungee comes tight, or at the sight of hundreds of feet of vertical ice or rock between your feet.

Climbing in general has become one of the primary release mechanisms for adventure lovers in the '90's, and ice climbing draws those who want to push their own physical and mental limits while at the same time challenging nature at its fiercest.

In the ten years since the first edition of this guide was published, the popularity of winter climbing in northern New England has grown tremendously. There are many more climbers, and many more climbs. While Frankenstein has always been popular, today the term "swarmed" might be more appropriate for the popular routes. Advances in technology have made the sport both more user-friendly, as well as significantly safer. Today's limits are defined not by what the equipment is capable of, but rather by what the climber is capable of. And those limits seem to be re-defined every season.

Ice climbing has always been an exhilerating way to experience the winter environment. The purpose of this guidebook is to give climbers the information they need to safely enjoy ice climbing in New England. To that end, we wish you good climbing.

Rick Wilcox
September, 1992

ACKNOWLEDGEMENTS

I had originally hoped to have this new guide available for the winter of 1991. Dollars being tight in the outdoor industry snd still feeling the financial impact of our successful 1991 Mount Everest expedition the project was delayed for one year.

Much information for this updated guide comes directly from the first edition and I would like to thank the following people for the time and energy they put into the 1982 guide:

Ed Webster — Mt. Washington Valley
Bill Supple — Camden
Chris Hassig — Baker River Valley
Bill Kane — Evans Notch
Matt Peer, Clint Cummins, John Embrie, Brinton Young, Dennis Drayna
    and Gustavo Brillembourg — Lake Willoughby

The new information for this new edition has come from many different people, and without their help it would have been an impossible task. Thanks especially to the following people for their enthusiastic help and support.

Dave Getchel Jr. — Camden
Bob Baribeau — Katahdin
Jim Shimberg — Baker River Valley
Bill Pelkey — Smuggler's Notch
Kevin Slater — Grafton Notch and Katahdin
Kurt Winkler — many areas
Todd Swain — many areas
Brad White — many areas
Bruce Luetters — maps

Special thanks to Peter Lewis who did all the editing, design, typesetting and production of this book. Peter spent the spring and summer of 1992 making this new guide happen. He had to organize all the new route information that accumulated at I.M.E. during the 1980's, combine it with the information from the first edition, and then bring it all together in a funcitonal design. Peter also ran down photographs of hard-to-find-areas and those special shots when the route was in its best condition. I look forward to working with Peter on future writing projects.

I would also like to extend my appreciation to George Hurley for his diligent work in going over the manuscript. Without his efforts, this book simply would not be worth reading.

Additionally, the Mount Washington Observatory, Appalachian Mountain Club, Baxter State Park Authority and Briggs Bunker provided key technical information..

Of course without the climbers, the informtaion in this guide would be non-existent. Their professional and concientious recording of events, times and climbs, and their sense of excitement and adventure gave this project vitality. Thanks to Bob Proudman, Doug Tescher, Steve Zajchowski, Rainsford Rouner, Mark Whiton, Dave Walters, Frank Lawrence, John Bouchard, Peter Cole, Dave Linden, Michael Hartrich, Mark Richey, Doug Madara, John Bragg, Al Rubin, Sam Streibert, Rich Mulhern, Doug Burnell, Paul Ross, Misha Kirk, Chris Hassig, Matt Peer, Steve Larson, David Stone, Bill Kane, Nick Yardley, Dave Karl, Marc Chauvin, Gerry Handren, Lee Stevens, John Tremblay, Chris Ellms, Bill Aughton, Bob Timmer, Ben Townsend, Bob Parrott, Rob Adair, Ted Hammond, Joe Lentini, Charlie Townsend, Randy Rackcliff, Dennis McKinnon, Paul Boissonneault, Henry Kendall, Gerry Handren, Ken Henderson, Kevin Codraro, Peter Hovling, Jeff Butterfield and many others.

Thanks also to all of the New England climbers who make this such a wonderful place to live.

Paul Boissonneault on WIDOW'S WALK, one of Frankenstein's most spectacular and elusive routes.

Photo by Steve Larson

C O N T E N T S

Chapter/area   Page

Chapter/area   Page

I N T R O D U C T I O N

T he endless march of high technology has transformed what was once a very serious undertaking into a popular and considerably safer winter sport. No longer do climbers in the Northeast have to hang up their ropes for the winter. The mountains of New England contain a vast number of quickly accessible frozen waterfalls, slides, and gully climbs that now can be climbed with the same confidence as any summer rock climb.

Unlike other ice climbing areas, New England always offersy ice in excellent condition somewhere, be it in Huntington Ravine, at Frankenstein Cliff or at Lake Willoughby. Come December first and often earlier the ice climbing season begins on Mount Washington and often lasts well into April offering excellent climbing at all grades for all types of ice climbers.

The process by which waterfall ice forms is so variable that no rule of thumb applies. Each winter presents a unique set of climactic variables. The amount and type of precipitation, wind velocity, temperature, freeze/thaw cycles, elevation, and the direction toward which the climb faces are all factors which effect the condition of a climb during any given winter. It takes a significant amount of mountaineering experience, research, intuition, and a healthy dose of common sense to be able to read the conditions of an ice climb or a snow slope. There are no short cuts to gaining this knowledge; simply put in your time in the mountains with an experienced partner.

Water ice forms in New England each year regardless of snowfall and by mid-winter, most areas are in good shape. Some routes, like those at Lake Willoughby, and the big routes on Cathedral and Cannon take sustained winter weather to form up well, and late January through February is the most popular time to climb the big routes. When these routes like THE BLACK DIKE, REPENTENCE, or THE LAST GENTLEMAN do come in, you had best be quick to take advantage of the situation because as little as 3-4 days of unseasonably mild temperatures can destroy months of ice build up.

The expression "patience is a virtue" seems appropriate to characterize the local attitude toward some of the extreme ice routes found in New England.

While the majority of routes are generally in shape for the duration of the season, there are a select group of climbs which form briefly, fleetingly, once each year or once a decade! The MYTH OF SISYPHUS is one prime example. It will tantalizingly form for a few hours each season, an inviting drip-line easily seen from North Conway, yet sometimes just a few minutes of sunshine are all it takes to bring it to the ground. In sixteen years it still has had less that a half-dozen ascents. For these routes, all we can say is wait, and be ready!

The purpose of this guide is not to document "every leaky drain" in New England. Given the vast frozen resources of the region, it would be an impossible task anyway. There will always be flows, tucked in here and there, that offer that wonderful combination of great climbing and adventure. The pioneering spirit cannot be squelched by guidebooks.

The purpose of this guide is to update the major activity since 1982, focusing on the popular areas, while at the same time introducing for the first time some superb climbing areas that are off the beaten path. A lot of time and research was dedicated to putting together the information you will find in the introductory section of the guide: the extensive chapter on history full of classic photos, a discussion of the notorious weather that can help make sense of the extremes, discussions of equipment and safety, etc. In addition the use of maps and charts, particularly those that begin the sections for each major area, have all been designed to help climbers appreciate their sport more, find their way efficiently throughout the areas covered, and enjoy the challenge of winter climbing as safely as possible.

It is certain that there will someday be a third edition of this guide. In order to be as accurate and thorough as possible in recording routes, we must rely on you, the climber, to provide us with the best information possible. Please send corrections or new route information to the address below. To insure that your information will be included, please provide all pertinent data: area, name of climb, relationship to existing routes, grade, approach and descent directions, route description, names of first ascent party and date, availability of photos, your address and phone number, etc. We appreciate your cooperation and look forward to hearing from you.

Rick Wilcox
International Mountain Equipment
Box 494, Main St.
North Conway, NH 03860

S A F E T Y

S afety cannot be over emphasized in ice climbing. Consider for a moment all the implements an ice climber carries on a climb. Ice axe, ice hammers, crampons, even ice screws are all sharp and potentially dangerous. Even a short fall on ice can result in serious injuries. A caught crampon can snap an ankle, an ice tool can inflict a nasty puncture wound. In rock climbing, the saying once was that the leader must not fall; on ice this concept is still important!

Ice climbing areas tend to be more isolated than most summer rock areas, so a rescue, should it be necessary, is not a matter of minutes away. In winter, many hours could pass between an accident and the arrival of the first rescuers. While winter temperatures hover at or below zero, this elapsed time becomes very critical indeed. Since an injured climber's body temperature will drop rapidly unless immediate insulation can be provided, an extra down jacket and pack with a built-in foam pad can literally become a lifesaver.

The Mountain Rescue Service (MRS) of New Hampshire was formed in 1972 to assist the local and state rescue organizations during technical rock and ice rescues. Prior to 1972, the Fish and Game Department, legally responsible for all rescue efforts in the state, would contact climbers from as far away as Massachusetts to come to the aid of other mountaineers. Fortunately, there were only a few technical rescues during those years.

At the present time, the MRS works in conjunction with a large number of other organizations including the Appalachian Mountain Club, the U.S. Forest Service, the State Police, and North Conway Rescue. A core of about twenty -five climbers make up the first response team, with many more in reserve if needed. The team is on call twenty-four hours a day year round, and is composed of highly qualified and dedicated local climbers. With twenty years of rescue experience, the team has become a cohesive and exemplary organization. In its role of assisting climbers in trouble, the MRS deserves the respect and continued support of all climbers, visitors, and residents.

By their very nature, technical rescues are extremely hazardous, especially in winter. Many climbing accidents are the consequence of objective, and hence, uncontrollable dangers: rockfall, avalanch, etc. That there are inherent dangers in climbing, no one can deny; a climber can only use good judgment and try to avoid them.

In January, 1982, Albert Dow, a seasoned member of the MRS and a professional climbing instructor for the EMS Climbing School, lost his life while on a rescue mission on Mt. Washington. During this period of extremely bad weather and high avalanche danger, all the team members were aware of the risks, yet persevered in searching for two ice climbers who had not returned from a trip into Huntington Ravine. After spending several days and nights out in below   -20°F

MRS members brave extreme weather near the summit of Mt. Washington during the rescue in which Albert Dow was killed.
Photo by David Stone

weather, the stranded climbers were found on the opposite side of the mountain and subsequently rescued by helicopter.

Many climbers recognize the risks to which the rescue members are exposed. Rescuers are volunteers in the purest sense. The decision to go, or not to go on a rescue, is based as much on personal safety as on the tremendous desire to help a fellow climber in trouble. If the risk is too great, the choice to stay home is understandable.

Before heading out into the mountains, each individual climber must try to accurately gauge his own preparedness, skill and judgement. The possibility of an accident must be realistically guaged, and the necessary equipment and skills for self-rescue should be in place long before before the climb begins. After such self-evaluation, this guide can assist you in locating a climb suited to your abilities.

I N S T R U C T I O N

I f you feel that you are lacking some of the necessary basic skills to be safe in the mountains in winter, or just want to polish up on the latest ice climbing techniques, then, by all means, seek out proper climbing instruction and guidance. Traditionally, climbers have learned their trade from fellow climbers. Organizations such as the Appalachian Mountain Club and the Harvard Mountaineering Club have sponsored trips into the White Mountains of northern New England since the 1920's, and many of today's great climbers got their start from such outings. Further information about AMC climbing programs may be obtained by writing to:

AMC
5   Joy Street
Boston, Massachusetts 02108

With today's faster lifestyles, others will prefer to learn ice climbing with a professional climbing school. The following guide services in the Mt. Washington Valley provide expert instruction in all aspects of climbing. Take advantage of their expertise. A few lessons will save you years of trial and error.

International Mountain Climbing School, Inc.
Box 1666
North Conway, NH 03860
AMGA acreditted
(603) 356-7013

Eastern Mountain Sports Climbing School, Inc.
Box 514
North Conway, NH 03860
AMGA acreditted
(603) 356-5433

Mountain Guides Alliance, Inc.
Box 266
North Conway, NH 03860
(603) 356-5310

George Hurley
RR 1, Box 99A
North Conway, NH 03860
AMGA certified
(603) 447-3086

Ice climbing, as Yvon Chouinard once described it, certainly is a slippery game. It is a sport where physical and mental preparedness are paramount, where only the best quality equipment should be used at all times, and even the slightest slip or break in concentration can lead to injury or worse. New England's mountains are beautiful and inspiring, with an atmosphere uniquely their own. We hope you always enjoy them in safety.

Nick Yardley, director of the International Mountain Climbing School, leads students up PEGASUS, a classic grade 3 route at Frankenstein.

Photo by S. Peter Lewis

W E A T H E R

The climate in northern New England is notoriously variable and old Yankee wisdom says "If you don't like the weather just wait a few minutes." In no other activity is that saying more relevant than winter climbing, where sudden changes in temperature, wind or visibility can turn a pleasant day's climbing into a nightmare struggle for survival. In far too many instances tragedy in New England's mountains can be linked to weather.

New England weather conditions are complicated by a number of geographic factors including: elevation, aspect (north facing, south facing, etc.) proximity to mountain ranges, etc. These determine what can be very site-specific weather conditions. Though ice climbing locales in New England are often geographically close, drastic differences can be seen between areas just a few minutes drive apart. For instance, it isn't unusual at all for the weather to be sunny, calm and 25^0, in North Conway, a perfect day for ice clmbing on Cathedral Ledge, while just twelve miles away in Crawford Notch it's overcast, windy and ten degrees cooler. And move just eight miles farther north and climb up 3,500 feet to Huntington Ravine on Mt. Washington and it can easily be near zero, with gale force winds and no visibility.

New England's winter weather is not to be underestimated. Each year there are climbers who get into trouble because the weather turns bad and they are not prepared. Mt. Washington is a major attraction for winter mountaineers in northern New England, yet almost every season lives are lost there, many a result of unexpected bad weather.

As an aid to understanding the complexities of northern New England winter weather, and planning for a day's climbing, the following chart gives data for three stations that cover some of the expected winter conditions from the relatively mild "valley" areas like North Conway, to the more harsh "notch" conditions such as in Pinkham Notch, to the severe weather common on "summit" areas like Mt. Washington. Throughout the book, in the introduction to each major area, a designation will be given ("valley", "notch" or "summit") depending on how the area's site-specific conditions line up with the standards on the chart. This in no way guarantees that a "valley" area will always be 20^0

warmer than a "summit" area. Temperature inversions can reverse this situation, but in typical weather patterns, the relative differences between the valleys, notches and summits are fairly consistent.

Of special interest to climbers planning to venture to the higher elevations of New England, particularly Mt. Washington in the White Mountains and Katahdin in northern Maine, is the role that extreme temperatures and wind velocitiy can play on any given day.

The summit observatory on Mt. Washington has recorded minimum temperatures ranging from -20⁰ in November and April to between -38⁰ and -47⁰ December through March.

Along with severe low temperatures, add an *average* daily wind velocity for the period of 42 mph and almost any prolonged outdoor activity becomes prohibitive.

Poking their summits into the winter jet stream, these areas have weather more akin to the arctic regions of Labrador and should be treated with extra caution. There are plenty of other places to climb on a bad day.

	Avg. High Temp. (^{o}F)	Avg. Low Temp.	Avg. Snow Fall (in.)
NOVEMBER			
N. Conway	46.7⁰	27.2⁰	6.7"
Pinkham Notch	41.0⁰	24.4⁰	19.5"
Mt. Washington	26.9⁰	13.8⁰	32.3"
DECEMBER			
N. Conway	33.1⁰	12.4⁰	22.5"
Pinkham Notch	28.3⁰	8.0⁰	30.6"
Mt. Washington	17.0⁰	1.2⁰	43.0"
JANUARY			
N. Conway	31.7⁰	9.0⁰	22.5"
Pinkham Notch	24.2⁰	2.8⁰	29.5"
Mt. Washington	13.4⁰	-3.3⁰	40.3"
FEBRUARY			
N. Conway	35.1⁰	10.1⁰	21.8"
Pinkham Notch	27.6⁰	6.2⁰	31.3"
Mt. Washington	13.1⁰	-3.4⁰	40.7"
MARCH			
N. Conway	41.8⁰	19.5⁰	16.4"
Pinkham Notch	36.9⁰	16.6⁰	25.2"
Mt. Washington	19.1⁰	4.7⁰	42.0"
APRIL			
N. Conway	54.0⁰	31.0⁰	6.4"
Pinkham Notch	48.7⁰	25.9⁰	16.3"
Mt. Washington	28.9⁰	15.9⁰	31.6"

NOTE:Each recording station utilized a different set of years to compute their data and therefore this chart is useful for general comparison only.

E Q U I P M E N T

For climbing ice, equipment generally plays a greater part in determining the speed, security, and at times, the severity of the ascent, than it does in rock climbing. The ice climber is a tool user; and so a discussion of hardware and software related to and designed for ice climbing is appropriate.

Hand tools can be grouped into six categories whether they are hammers or axes:

With practice, a single swing of the ice axe may be all that is necessary to make a superb handhold.

Photo by S. Peter Lewis

1) Straight-picked alpenstocks, still in use as walking axes.

2) Natural arc tools which are designed for a number of uses from glacier travel in longer lengths to models with short handles and teeth the length of the pick for steep ice.

3) Steeply drooped tools designed for steep ice and used with a more downward hooking swing.

4) Reverse-curve picks which are placed with a more naturally arcing swing but offer a secure feeling similar to a drooped tool.

5) Tubular-picked tools which offer superb penetration in all ice conditions without overly shattering the surrounding ice. They are more fragile than other picks and so not as functional for verglassed or alpine routes, nor do they hook as well.

6) A sixth design is characterized by a curved shaft that is designed to allow the hands a more naturally aligned grip. In addition it reduces the tendancy to knuckle bash, and changes the swing dynamics to more of a flip, which works particularly well with reverse curve picks. Tools with curved shafts are best suited to the harder, steeper routes.

Hammers come with heads for pounding in ice pitons while axes are fitted with an adze that has any number of uses from cutting the occasional step and enlarging belay ledges, to clearing rotten ice for solid screw placements and cutting bollards for rappel anchors. Several styles of adze, from the traditional straight blade, to curved "scoops" and even tubular designs are available.

No matter which type of tool one chooses, it is important to understand that confidence and familiarity are the factors governing how well a climber performs with a given axe or hammer. Choose hand tools designed for the type of climbs you intend to do and get used to the way they feel when properly placed and removed. Also remember that no tool is meant to be bashed (con-

sistently) into rocks, trees, or frozen turf and that this kind of treatment often re-sults in a shorten-ing of the pick at very inopportune moments. As a pre-caution against a re-treat or worse, most climbers carry a third tool for use if one of the other tools is dropped or broken. A spare pick is also a good to have along.

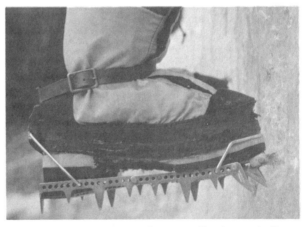

Well placed crampon front points, even if only penetrating a quarter of an inch, can give a secure purchase.
Photo by Joe Lentini

Crampons can be divided into two classes, flexible and rigid. Anyone climbing ice should be using 12 point crampons as there is nothing you can do with 10 point crampons that you can't also do with 12 point crampons, but there is much that can be done with 12 points that is impossible armed with only a set of 10 points.

The advantages of flexible crampons are that they will flex somewhat when used on mountain boots and hence are more comfortable for glacier travel. When they are used on a rigid ice boot, they will provide security somewhat like a rigid crampon, although some flex as well as vibration will always be present. In alpine climbing the flexible crampon provides a bit more "feel" on rock than do rigid crampons.

These two basic crampon types are further separated into either step-in (requiring a substantial welt on the boot) or strap-on, which can be used on any mountaineering boot. The advantages of the step-in design are many: they typically fit the boot tighter and with less play; they do not constrict the boot upper at all and so do not interfere with circulation; they can be put on or taken off in a matter of seconds; which can be critical at 20 below, and once on, they do not have the tendancy to loosen as do strap-on crampons. Both rigid as well as flexible crampons are available with excellent step-in designs.

For most climbing in New England where the ice is typically hard and steep, rigid crampons are the best choice, and for pure vertical front pointing, they are the only choice. When fitting crampons, either flexible or rigid, they should fit snugly to the sole of the boot, with front points clearing the toe of the boot by 3/4"-1 1/4". Always keep the screws tight and the points sharp.

Ice protection comes in two basic styles: tubular screws which are screwed into and out of the ice and (traditionally) offer the greatest security, and tubular pitons such as Lowe Snargs which are driven in and then screwed out of the ice. Placing of these screws is easier when a hole has been started with an axe pick (tube picks work great for this). A third design, which looks like the pick of a reverse curve axe, is designed to be pounded in and offers reasonable security. This style is especially useful in thin ice where nothing else really works very well.

The ice climber's wardrobe is one of personal preference, but there are also certain points that should be made about how to dress for cold activities. The layering principle is very important to climbers because they go through periods of extreme effort when less clothing is needed, to times of rest (belaying) when many layers may be needed to keep warm.

The ability to adjust to this temperature variation is very important for both comfort and safety. The first layer should be wool or synthetic (polypropylene) underwear. (Cotton is not an effective layer in a winter layering system.) Then come the layers of wool, pile, or Thinsulate garments. Over those, use a wind shell or mountain parka of nylon, 60/40 cloth, or gore-Tex, any one of which is windproof; but, only the gore-Tex is waterproof.

Layering is also important for the hands and feet. Thin polypropylene sox, often followed by a vapor barrier liner and then a heavy wool sock is the standard for feet while polypropylene gloves followed by wool gloves and finaly a gor-tex shell complete the system for the hands. Wool hats and balaclavas are usually enough for keeping the head warm with the addition of a parka or shell hood in very cold weather. The importance of wearing a helmet as protection from falling ice is critical, and they do offer some additional insulation. Extras which should always be in a pack are a pile or wool sweater, down jacket, wind pants, rain pants and an extra hat and gloves. (Rain parkas are extremely important in New England as it can be very wet and cold).

One piece "flight suits" made up of an insulating/windproof combination offer a lighter weight, more flexible, and warmer alternative to traditional top and bottom layering. They have become very popular in recent years and are especially adapted to the very cold environment of northern New England.

The evolution of ice climbing equipment over the last decade has made for great changes in boot designs. In the late 1970's the only choice for winter climbers in New England was either a leather double boot, or a single leather boot worn with a supergator. By the early 1980's Koflach had introduced its first plastic double boot. Lighter, warmer, waterproof, extremely rigid, and de-signed to work in conjunction with step-in crampons and supergators, these boots caught on immediately with New England climbers and just a few years later had eclipsed leather boots for technical ice climbing. Perhaps their only disadvantage is a loss of "feel" for the rock on alpine routes. Leather still out-performs plastic on some mixed terrain.

Finally we'd like to add some items that we feel are important additions to a climber's sack whether one is headed to Mt. Washington for a day or Katahdin for a week. A headlamp which works should always be in your pack as should a compass. Both can help you find your way out when you've miscalculated or had bad luck. A bit of food and water, (dehydration is a major cause of hypothermia) a nylon "space-blanket," and some matches or a lighter can transform a bivy from a "death camp" into just an uncomfortable night. A small first aid kit is also a good idea and should contain some heat packs along with the standard supplies. Chemical heat packs placed in the armpits and groin of an injured climber can help tremendously in offsetting the effects of hypothermia. Beyond these personal preferences, judgment will determine which items you will or won't need.

Equipment has come a long way in the last decade, and there is no doubt that more advances are on the way. Ten years from now we may find ourselves saying "how in the world did we ever go climbing dressed like that?" Today's climber, fitted head to toe with the best equipment can step out into the winter world with confidence. Yet equipment can never be a substitute for experience and sound judgement. Since the very beginning, climbers have carried the most important piece of equipment under their helmets.

What a difference ten years makes! The contrast between these two photos could not be more dramatic. Both Rainsford Rouner on DROPLINE (left) and Dave Karl on MINDBENDER (below) are representative of climbers on the hardest routes of their generations. But fashion trends not withstanding, the evolution of equipment is dramatically illustrated in the comparison. All of Dave's equipment, from his re-curved ice tool picks and step-in crampons, right down to his plastic boots and one-piece gore-tex suit, indicate the radical changes in design that ice climbing equipment has gone through since the early 1980's. Who knows, maybe in another ten years we'll be chuckling at Dave's clothing and equipment.

Photo by Rick Wilcox

Photo by Ted Hammond

R A T I N G S

Rating ice climbs has always been a slippery affair. Unlike rock climbs, which, save for the occasional flake disappearing, remain virtually unchanged from season to season, the difficulty of a given ice route is entirely dependent on its condition. And that is affected by a number of factors: thick or thin, mush or bulletproof, hacked up or smooth, and the list goes on. Because of this, by definition, ice ratings are subjective, and the grades given are best viewed as generalizations. It is unlikely that you will ever see an ice grade broken down into a, b,c,d as in rating rock. Pluses and minuses are about as exact as the ice will allow, and that only on routes that come in consistently each year.

As a rule, the technical grades given in this guide are representative of the climb in its "typical" mid-season condition, and on a day with average weather conditions. Below zero temperatures, high winds or heavy snowfall can add a full grade or more to a given route, while a sunny day with the thermometer in the 40's can make a hard climb feel easy. And on climbs with only one ascent, the rating is purely subjective and subsequent ascents may alter it radically.

Other factors that should be taken into account that are not included in the over-all grade are approaches and descents. Adding a three mile thrash through pucker brush to a three pitch grade 3 route increases the commitment dramatically. For example, while ELEPHANT'S HEAD GULLY in Crawford Notch, and POINT in the Madison Gulf are both given the overall grade of II 3+, the fact is that the approach to ELEPHANT'S HEAD GULLY takes thirty seconds while getting to the Madison Gulf entails a six mile thrash through deep snow that has been described by veteran bushwhacker Todd Swain as "the most horrendous I've ever experienced. Five times worse than Huntington's." It is wise therefore to take the entire trip from car to car, and not just the technical rating,into consideration when planning a day's climbing.

Up until the late 1970's technical grades for ice climbs could best be described as vague. In Peter Cole and Rick Wilcox's first ice guide to the area, **Shades of Blue**, published in 1976, climbs were simply graded "easy," "moderate" and "hard." By the late '70's with many more climbers active there was a real need for an accurate rating system to compare the levels of difficulty and commitment of the increasing number of climbs in the region. Local climber Rick Wilcox adapted the Scottish ice grading system, a simple numerical scale from 1-4, and called it the New England Ice Scale or NEI for short. (Climbers had casually been using such a system for years, but it had never been nailed down.) A fifth grade was soon added and, with the additions of pluses and minuses, the relative accuracy and simplicity of the scale has helped it endure.

During the early 1980's ice climbing continued to grow in popularity. The first edition of *An Ice Climber's Guide to Northern New England*, which appeared in 1982, was the first place that the NEI system was published. It was quickly accepted by the climbing community.

In the following years, the simplicity of the system and its reliability as a purely technical grading system was demonstrated by the adaptation of similar systems across the U.S. and Canada. In areas such as the Canadian Rockies, (where the length and difficulty of the climbs can be greater than in New England, grade 6 was added for such 1980's testpieces as POLAR CIRCUS and a seventh grade came a few years later with the ascents of such horror shows as TERMINATOR and REALITY BATH (The latter put up by New England local Randy Rackliff with Marc Twight) By a consensus of local climbers, the grade 6 or 7 is considered to be above the scope of any New England ice route in terms of length and commitment. Therefore, the ice rating of 5+ distinguishes the hardest ice climbs in this region. (Kurt Winkler's ascent of LA POMME D'OR in Quebec in the mid 1980's was the first ice climb in this part of North America to be graded a 6)

John Tremblay doing what he does best, pushing the limits, this time at Pitcher Falls.
Photo by Joe Lentini

In Europe at this time a similar system was adapted for pure ice routes, and by the early 1990's a climber would find that a Grade 5 route in Canada, New Hampshire, and France would all be comparable in terms of describing the technical difficulties of the ice. Obviously length and commitment could differ radically, fortunately there are other recognized standards to describe these factors. Since the system of grading technical ice difficulty is now almost universally accepted, the "NEI" designation has been dropped from the descriptions in this guidebook.

The following climbs are thought to be classic climbs of the rating system and best illustrate the transition in difficulty from one grade to another. All grades are technical and require the use of ropes, belays and ice climbing equipment.

GRADE 1

Low angle water ice less than 50^0 or long, moderate snow climbs requiring a basic level of technical expertise for safety: WILLEY'S SLIDE (Crawford Notch), CENTRAL GULLY (Huntington Ravine).

GRADE 2

Low angle water ice routes with short bulges up to 60^0: CINEMA GULLY (Mt. Willard), YALE GULLY (Huntington Ravine).

GRADE 3

Steeper water ice of 50^0-60^0 with short 70^0-90^0 bulges: PINNACLE GULLY (Huntington Ravine), STANDARD ROUTE (Frankenstein Cliff)

GRADE 4

Short, vertical columns interspersed with rests on 50^0-60^0 ice. Fairly sustained climbing. DRACULA (Frankenstein Cliff), TWENTY BELOW ZERO GULLY (Lake Willoughby), WATERFALL GULLY (Katahdin).

GRADE 5

Generally multi-pitch ice climbs with sustained difficulties and/or strenuous vertical columns with little rest possible: REPENTENCE (Cathedral Ledge), THE LAST GENTLEMAN (Lake Willoughby).

5+ Multi-pitch ice routes with a heightened degree of seriousness, long vertical sections, and extremely sustained difficulties - the hardest ice climbs in New England to date: REMISSION (Cathedral Ledge), THE PROMENADE (Lake Willoughby), OMEGA (Cannon Cliff), MAINLINE (Mt. Kineo).

THE COMMITMENT GRADE

In addition to the pure technical grade the international system for commitment is used throughout the guide and is designated by a Roman numeral just before the technical grade. This grade represents the amount of time a competent party can expect to spend on a given climb under normall conditions. Again, particularly foul weather, or a route in bad conditions, can affect this grade as well. And, as mentioned before, approaches and descents should also be figured into the equation. The following breakdown will help you determine your choice of routes.

I Up to several hours.

II About half a day.

III A full day, up to seven or eight hours.

IV A substantial undertaking; a very long day, possibly including a bivouac.

V A big wall climb of 1-2 days; could be done in a single day by a very fit team.

VI Multi-day big wall climbs over two days.

VII Big wall ascents in remote alpine situations.

(Note: there are currently no grade VI or VII ice climbs in New England.)

H I S T O R Y

Technical ice climbing in New England has heen recorded as far back as 1894. On December 26th of that year, Dr. R.C. Larrabee, Herschel C. Parker, and a Mr. Andrew attempted to climb the headwall of Tuckerman Ravine. Unfortunately, their efforts were foiled by the large amount of ice they encountered. Not to be deterred so easily, Parker returned alone on February 27th, 1895, and completed the first recorded ascent of the Tuckerman Ravine headwall. On his successful ascent he carried an ice axe, a useful piece of equipment he'd neglected to bring the first time.

As early as 1915 Howard Jackson and Frank S. Mason had been working on boot and crampon designs to use in the White Mountains. They had rejected Swiss crampons because they felt they were too heavy and wouldn't work properly on soft-soled boots. The Swiss crampons were designed to be worn with thick leather soles. Even so, some early New England climbers felt that the crampons would conduct too much heat away from the foot, increasing the danger of frostbite. Jackson and Mason's solution was a boot with a thick leather welt which held the metal spikes in place and protected the climber's feet from the extreme cold characteristic of New England winters. Their design, while adequate for winter hikers, failed to satisfy the needs of technical climbers. European equipment, although not as warm as the Jackson-Mason design, simply performed better on water ice.

During the early years of New England ice climbing, all recorded activity centered in Huntington Ravine on Mount Washington's east flank. Not until the 1950's did the focus begin to shift to other areas of New England.

The first technical winter ascent in Huntington Ravine was made on February 23, 1927, when A.J. Holden and N.L. Goodrich climbed CENTRAL GULLY, the easiest of the six main gullies in the ravine. The second ascent of CENTRAL GULLY was done a year later on February 12, 1928. J.C. Hurd, Noel E. Odell, B. Bronson, C.W. Linscotte, K.D. McCutchen, N.W. Spadavecchia, R.S. Sperry, L.S. Southwich, and Daniel Underhill left the Glen House at 7:30 A.M. on snowshoes. After a quick trip up to the ravine, they donned crampons for the ascent of The Fan. At the base of CENTRAL GULLY, the party roped up for the ascent, and with Hurd and Underhill in the lead, reached the Alpine Garden by 1:30 P.M. No protection was used on the climb, but steps were cut up a difficult icy slab, the crux of the route.

On March 16, 1928, Noel Odell, J.C. Hurd, Lincoln O'Brien, and Robert L.M. Underhill returned to Huntington Ravine with a new objective, the wide prominent gully now known as ODELL'S GULLY. The climb proved substantially harder than CENTRAL GULLY. Although the three climbers were roped together and belayed, not one ice screw was used for protection. The June, 1929 issue of *Appalachia* contained an interesting note, predicting that for the future of ice climbing on Mt. Washington, "apparently nothing remained to be done."

Hardly had the print dried when Samuel A. Scoville and Julian H. Whittlesey made the first ascent of PINNACLE GULLY, certainly one of the most famous ice climbs in New England. Earlier attempts by the leading climbers of the day, O'Brien, Underhill and others had been unsuccessful, their attempts usually cut short by darkness. Scoville and Whittlesey were far from being the best climbers, in fact they were rank novices. But they did posess the one quality that has so often been evident in climbing history, in today's parlance they were willing to "go for it." Reflecting on the climb years later, Whittlesey admitted cheerfully to historians Guy and Laura Waterman that not only was it the hardest climb he had ever done, but that PINNACLE GULLY was "the only one" he had ever done. Their remarkably fast one

Jullian Whittlesey in 1992
Photo courtesy
Jullian Whittlesey

day ascent of the gully, the hardest of the Huntington Ravine gullies, was a landmark climb. During the next five years, the proficiency and skill of these first climbers were proven time and time again; it wasn't until the fifth ascent of the route by W.V. Graham and Matthew and James C. Maxtwell in March, 1948, that PINNACLE GULLY was repeated in a single day! Another interesting bit of history concerning PINNACLE GULLY occured on the second ascent on March 30, 1934, by Alan Wilcox and Wiliam M. House. They completed the climb with ten-point crampons and again didn't use a single ice screw for protection. Ice climbers of this era, obviously men of uncommon mettle, usually carried steel carabiners in their pockets for occasional use at belays.

In late March, 1941, an attempt was made by a party consisting of Wiliam P. House, Kenneth A. Henderson, Maynard Malcolm Miller, and Andrew J. Kaufman to climb the left-hand of the two northern gullies in Huntington Ravine. The attempt, however, was cut short by a storm, approaching darkness, and difficult conditions. Thus, the gully which had handed them defeat was appropriately named DAMNATION GULLY. The following winter, Maynard Miller and William Latady climbed NORTH GULLY, neighboring DAMNATION. Then on January 31, 1943, William Putnam and Andrew J. Kaufman returned to complete the first succcssful ascent of DAMNATION GULLY — the last gully in Huntington Ravine to feel the swing of the climber's ice axe.

Maynard Miller and Andrew Kaufman cutting steps up North Gully in 1941.
Photo by Kenneth A. Henderson

Until the 1950's all ice climbs in New England were credited to members of either the Harvard Mountaineering Club or the Appalachian Mountain Club. As a result, lessons in ice climbing were to be had only from either of these two climbing organizations. However, the pace of winter climbing activity was remarkably uneven. During the 1920's and 30's, the AMC had regularly scheduled trips to Mount Washington, yet, between 1933-1954, not a single visit was scheduled. The twenty-one year hiatus ended in March, 1954, when twenty-five people participated in an AMC ice climbing trip to the White Mountains. A healthy interest was subsequently rekindled in the sport and the AMC has sponsored such trips ever since.

Although the precise date of the first ascent of Willey's Slide in Crawford Notch is not known, it is known that climbing trips to the area commenced as early as 1954. Finally, after over 60 years of technical climbing in the gullies of Mount Washington, climbers began to turn to the multitude of other ice-laced crags and gullies in the White Mountains to enliven their sport and seek new directions. One of the next major winter ascents accomplished in the region occured on February 7, 1954, when David Bernays and Andrew Griscom, members of the Harvard Mountaineering Club, made the first winter ascent of STANDARD ROUTE on Whitehorse Ledge. Their seven hour climb involved several tricky sections, including a pendulum over the infamous "brown spot" and some direct aid in the final overlaps. Surprisingly, it was another ten years before Cathedral Ledge, just a few hundred yards north of Whitehorse, was climbed in winter.

On January 19, 1964, Hugo Stadtmuller and Henry W. Kendall climbed the STANDARD ROUTE up Cathedral in difficult verglas conditions. Their ascent of the notorious "cave wall" ushered in a new level of difficulty in mixed climbing. In that same year, April, 1964, tragedy struck

Hugo Stadtmuller on the first winter ascent of STANDARD ROUTE on Cathedral Ledge.
Photo by Henry W. Kendall

the New England ice climbing community for the first time. John Griffen and Hugo Stadtmuller, both experienced climbers, failed to return to the Harvard Cabin after a day's ice climbing in Huntington Ravine. John Porter, who was staying at the cabin, reported to Ranger Richard Goodwin that his friends were overdue. The next morning, a joint Forest Service and AMC rescue team hurried into the Ravine where they found evidence of a massive avalanche which originated in CENTRAL GULLY. The climbers, whose bodies were uncovered at the base of The Fan, were apparently at the junction of CERNTRAL and PINNACLE GULLIES when the slide occured.

A year later, another fatal ice climbing accident occured in Huntington Ravine on March 14, 1965. Daniel Doody, a member of the successful 1963 American Everest Expedition, and Craig Merrihue fell from near the top of PINNACLE GULLY. A corkscrew-type ice screw found clipped to the climbing rope was assumed to be the belay piton. When the leader fell, the belay failed and both climbers fell 800 feet down the length of the gully to the rocks of The Fan below.

As the preceding accidents point out, ice climbing up until the late 1960's was an all-too-insecure, dangerous, and slippery game. Prior to 1968, the standard technique for ice climbing was to chop a ladder of steps up the slope. Ten-point hinged crampons, long-shafted straight-pick ice axes, and a handful of ice screws were the climber's standard gear. The introduction of nylon rope in 1947 had increased greatly the margin of safety, but ice climbing was still a dangerously precarious sport. Standards of difficulty were not rising during these years. But in the late 1960's, an American hardware manufacturer set out to revolutionize the sport.

Yvon Chouinard travelled to Europe, climbing in Chamonix, France, the center of European climbing. There, climbers were using rigid 12-point crampons and short ice axes and hammers with steeply drooped picks. Without cutting steps, and with an economy of energy, climbers frontpointed quickly up steep faces of neve ice. Two hand tools, an alpine hamer in one hand and short axe in the other, afforded them much greater stability and security. After a particularly successful alpine season in 1968, Chouinard returned to the U.S. with some grand plans. In his Ventura, California, machine shop, he produced the first American-designed, rigid, 12-point crampons, alpine hammers, and ice axes. Made in Europe to his specifications, Chouinard's new ice gear hit the New England ice climbing scene in the winter of 1969. Equipped with drooped tools and rigid crampons, climbers could now ascend even the

steepest ice without having to resort to the laborious techniques of step cutting. Almost overnight, new ice climbing areas in New England, once thought to contain ice much too steep to consider climbing, became approachable. Armed with these latest technological weapons, New England ice climbers began to scour the cliffs

A professional climber for over three decades, George Hurley remains one of the area's most respected climbers, seen here on the classic route CHIA at Frankenstein.

Photo by S. Peter Lewis

with renewed intensity, pushing the limits higher than ever before.

In the winter of 1969-70, Jim McCarthy headed north to try out his new ice equipment on Mount Washington. On February 1, 1970, he along with Bill Putnam, Rick Wilcox, Rob Wallace, and Carl Brandon made the first ascent of PINNACLE GULLY without cutting a single step. Their ascent proved once and for all that steep water ice could be climbed swiftly, surely, and safely with proper use of the new gear and the frontpointing technique. The entire party reached the Alpine Garden in under five hours.

The new technology that Chouinard developed not only made the standard routes easier and safer, but opened up a whole new world of possibilities. Areas that had always been passed over because they were obviously too difficult, could now be explored with confidence.

During the same season as PINNACLE GULLY's first step-less ascent,

John Bouchard on the second ascent of THE BLACK DIKE in 1973.
Photo by Rick Wilcox

Sam Streibert and Al Rubin discovered the unbelievable ice climbing potential at Frankenstein Cliff in Crawford Notch. The classic frozen waterfall, STANDARD ROUTE, was climbed first, then CHIA and PEGASUS the next year. Word soon spread of this fantastic ice climbing area, with its short approach, variety of routes, and relative lack of objective dangers.

It was during this time as well that Vermont's Smuggler's Notch began to see high caliber activity, initially spearheaded by Dave Cass and Phill Koch.

In an article in the 1971 issue of *Ascent* the Sierra Club mountaineering journal, Yvon Chouinard singled out THE BLACK DIKE on Cannon Cliff in Franconia Notch as one of the last unclimbed "plums" on the East Coast. Excitement mounted as climbers wondered who would accept Chouinard's challenge of "a black, filthy, horrendous icicle 600 feet high. Unclimbed." It didn't take long. Much to everyone's surprise, the first ascent was made by a young ice climber, John Bouchard, on December 18, 1971. His ascent was an epic in every sense of the word. On the first pitch his rope jammed, so he dropped it. Then the pick on his axe broke, and he dropped a mitten. Just as darkness was about to overtake him, Bouchard clawed his way to the woods, completing what even today is considered one of the most impressive individual accomplishments in New England climbing. To remove any doubt regarding his first ascent, Bouchard returned the following winter with Henry Barber, John Bragg, and Rick Wilcox to climb THE DIKE a second time. THE BLACK DIKE, the first ice climb in the region to be graded 5, was undeniably a major ascent in the history of New England ice climbing.

Soon afterwards, new ice routes of all grades of difficulty were recorded throughout the area. At the same time, ice climbing possibilities were investigated at Mt. Katahdin in northern Maine, a mountain whose remoteness and severe winter weather attracts only serious mountaineers. John Porter, Jeff Wood, Larry Hodin, and Dave Isles ascended a major new line, the GALLERY ROUTE, the first winter route up the South Basin Headwall's West Face during the 1972-73 season. Following this came the first ascent of the WATERFALL ROUTE by Bob Proudman and Mark Lawrence, one of a number of their first ascents in the South Basin area. Also on Katahdin, Dave Cilley and Henry Barber ascended a long, narrow ribbon of ice, the CILLEY-BARBER ROUTE, almost directly to the summit of Baxter Peak.

John Bragg on the first ascent of REPENTENCE in 1973.
Photo by Rick Wilcox

Back on Frankenstein Cliff, activity also began to increase. John Bragg and Wilcox ascended SMEAR, Bragg and A.J. LaFleur climbed

DRACULA, and Al Rubin and Oriel Sola-Costa did the WATERFALL. On Humphrey's Ledge, Rick Wilcox, Peter Cole, and A.J. LaFleur made it up BLACK PUDDING GULLY for the first time.

The culmination of the 1972-73 season was undoubtedly John Bragg and Rick Wilcox' first winter ascent of REPENTENCE on Cathedral Ledge, an ice climb now ranked among the finest in all of North America. A modern ice climber's test piece, REPENTENCE was the second ice climb in New England to be granted a rating of 5. As testimony to its difficulty and significance, an ascent of REPENTENCE today is still considered a major accomplishment and for many aspiring climbers it remains a route to be dreamed of.

Each winter to follow brought new ice climbers to the forefront and new areas in which to climb. In northern Vermont, a new area, as yet unclimbed, took on appeal and challenge. The flanks of Mt. Pisgah above Lake Willoughby promised routes steeper and colder than most others. Mike Hartrich, Al Rubin, and Henry Barber were the first to accept the challenge, ascending the appropriately named, TWENTY BELOW ZERO GULLY. Also, in Vermont, Smuggler's Notch provided John Bouchard and Steve Zajchowski, then students at the University of Vermont, with as many new routes as they could systematically climb.

The big climb at Frankenstein in 1973-74 was the first ascent of the BRAGG-PHEASANT, a series of thinly-iced runnels on the Main Cliff. John Bouchard, Steve Zajchowski, and Roger Martin added yet another NEI 5 to Cannon Cliff in December, 1975, by climbing the ice ribbon of FAFNIR, just to the right of THE BLACK DIKE. The crux was a section of difficult mixed climbing at the top of the flow.

A new and more aggressive group of climbers arrived during this

Michael Hartrich on the first ascent of TWENTY BELOW ZERO GULLY at Lake Willoughby.

Photo by Henry Barber

season, and many of the last big unclimbed lines fell to their determined efforts. At Cathedral Ledge, Rainsford Rouner, his brother, Tim, and Peter Cole made the long sought after winter ascent of REMISSION, the sister ice route to REPENTENCE. Although the first ascent team used etriers and direct aid on the column, it is done without aid today.

February, 1976, was one of those rare months in the history of any ice climbing area when the combination of exceptionally good conditions and a talented core group mix to produce a string of superior climbs. On Frankenstein Cliff, Rainsford Rouner, Peter Cole, and Rick Wilcox climbed the impressive icicle, DROPLINE (grade 4) and on Humphrey's Ledge, Mark Richey and Rainsford Rouner managed a quick ascent of THE SENATOR (grade 5), an ephemeral ice route which has never again returned .

Several of the routes climbed during this month were in the same, rare condition. Michael Hartrich and Mark Whiton made the first winter ascent of THIN AIR on Cathedral Ledge climbing ice all the way; over on the South Buttress of Whitehorse Ledge, the Rouner brothers ascended the MYTH OF SISYPHUS, a beautiful line which has also seldom formed again. On Cannon Cliff, the ice was also in unusually good "nick," and John Bouchard and Rainsford Rouner were quick to take advantage of this opportunity. Their superb climb, OMEGA (grade 5+), is considered to be the hardest ice route on Cannon and ranks also among the finest in the region. As in the case of all of the previously mentioned routes, OMEGA is rarely in good condition, and has been repeated infrequently.

An increased interest in a long neglected ice climbing area and a new trend in winter climbing both occurred in the winter of 1976-77. Noteworthy winter ascents were made of the difficult aid climbs on Cathedral Ledge, including Bryan Becker and Alain Comeau's ascent of MORDOR WALL. They seiged the climb over a period of three days, wisely preferring to bivouac in town! Earlier, with Eric Engberg, they had warmed up with a winter ascent of MINES OF MORIA. Comeau and Tony Trocchi also climbed CATHEDRAL DIRECT, finishing up the ice-choked upper chimney. Later, Doug Madara and Trocchi did DIEDRE, finding difficult mixed and artificial climbing on the route.

Over on the icy flanks of Mt. Pisgah above Lake Willoughby in Vermont, the golden age was just beginning. The Rouner brothers, Rainsford and Tim, in impeccable style, climbed the centerpiece of that area, THE LAST GENTLEMAN (NEI 5) in December, 1976. The Rouners returned the next month

Dave Karl on the incredibly steep and sustained crux of THE PROMENADE.
Photo by Ted Hammond

with Peter Cole to do battle with THE PROMENADE (grade 5+), a terrifyingly steep ice flow immediately to the right of the former route. Members of the Harvard Mountaineering Club were also active at Lake Willoughby doing numerous arm-destroying climbs. The principle climbers involved in the action were Clint Cummins, John Imbrie, Brinton Young, Dennis Drayna, and Gustavo Brillembourg. Some of their best efforts are classic routes of the Lake, among them are PLUG AND CHUG, MINDBENDER, and CRAZY DIAMOND.

A variety of other unique and noteworthy new ice routes were climbed in that same winter of 1976-77 as activity grew in scope to encompass nearly all ice climbing areas in New England. Bill Kane and Doug Madara completed the first winter ascent of THE GIRDLE OF WHITEHORSE LEDGE. Matt Peer, Danny Costa, Doug Strickholm, and Alec Behr were the main explorers of the Madison Gulf of Mt. Adams. In the winter of 1977-78, Jim Dunn, the master of hard, free rock climbs in the Mt. Washington Valley, garnered a few short, steep ice routes, particularly, GREAT MADNESS (then called by the uninspiring name of GULLY #3) at Mt. Willard, ANGEL CAKE on Frankenstein, and WAY IN THE WILDERNESS off the Kancamaugus Highway. The latter route, a steep ribbon east of Rainbow Slabs on the Painted Walls, was climbed with Peter Cole and Michael Hartrich.

Late that same winter, Bill Kane and Kim Smith climbed WHITE'S GULLY on White's Ledge in Bartlett. Also that year saw Cummins and Imbrie make the long trek to northern Maine where on the face of Mt. Kineo, overlooking Moosehead Lake, they climbed MAINELINE, a tremendously steep route that was as hard as it was spectacular. MAINELINE unfortunately suffered from the "out of sight, out of mind" syndrome and few took the six hour drive to follow in their footsteps.

As the 1970's drew to a close, the fury of activity that had made this perhaps the most important decade in the history of the sport, ebbed. With almost all of the major lines now established, the question was "what next?", but the answer was not obvious. With climbs rated at 5+, and no clearly harder lines to be found, the advance of pure technical difficulty came to a virtual standstill. Even today, over ten years later, the hardest technical grade in New England still stands at 5+.

The Waterman's have defined the period of the late 1970's and 1980's as "primarily one of consolidation...and perfection of style." With some of the psychological barriers of the unknown broken by the ascent of the hardest routes, and with the ongoing evolution of equipment, the high standards established by a handful of climbers in the '70's now became reachable for the masses.

With the fearsom reputation of routes such as the BLACK DIKE and RE-PENTENCE somewhat mellowed, ascents became commonplace, and a nice Saturday at Cannon could see several parties queued up for the DIKE, where just a few years before, only the hardmen dared tread.

Frankenstein and Huntington became more like playgrounds than ever and by the mid 1980's it wasn't uncommon to see nearly every popular route occupied on a nice winter day.

As the popularity of ice climbing increased, any icy drip in New England became fair game. "The modern age of ice climbing had permeated every piece of frozen verticality in the Northeast" reported the Watermans.

The GEOGRAPHIC FACTOR, one of the hardest routes in the Baker River Valley.
Dave Karl collection

The answer to "where next" really boiled down to "how next," and though the early 1980's saw many routes of tremendous difficulty put up such as REIGN OF TERROR by Matt Peer and Tom Dickey at Lake Willoughby, and the incredibly steep GEOGRAPHIC FACTOR, by Brian Bodeur, Tim Gotwols and Chris Hassig at Rattlesnake Mountain in the Baker River Valley, these routes tended to be shorter and though unquestionably hard, were not breakthroughs in the sense that climbs like THE BLACK DIKE or REPENTENCE had been. While those pushing the limits in the late 1970's developed techniques for overcoming relentless verticality such as hanging from wrist loops, hanging from their tools to place protection and in some instances (first ascent of REMISSION) even employing etriers, the 1980's would see a reversal of this trend with climbers finding the challenge in completing the hardest routes in the purest style.

Unlike the nearly naked rock climbers of today with their slippers, chalk bag and rack of quick draws, ice climbers by necessity are "tool users" who depend to a much greater degree on their equipment to engineer their way up a climb. Thus the definition of "good style" in ice climbing has always been somewhat vague. Everyone agrees that not using etriers is more pure than using them, and that placing protection without hanging from the tools is more pure than hanging. In a sport festooned with gear, the philosophy that the less you use, the better, gradually began to take hold.

A leading practitioner of this trend toward purer style was longtime North Conway guide Kurt Winkler, whose list of ascents in the best of style was rivaled by few and inspiring to many. With Ed Webster in 1982 he made the first complete ascent of the mystical Rouner route THE MYTH OF SISYPHUS on Whitehorse ledge, a delicate hollow runnel that narrowed and steepened to vertical 400 feet off the deck. But it was his ascent with Alec Behr and Joe Lentini

Kurt Winkler leading the scary second pitch of EAGLE"S GIFT.

Photo by Joe Lentini

of EAGLE'S GIFT in Glen, N.H., that was representative of the opportunities for development in the mid 1980's. Though only two short pitches long, the climb was horrendously thin and poorly protected. After sixty feet of verglass the second pitch followed a fractured detached runnel only a couple of feet wide, and demanded a delicate, controlled style radically different from the full-on bashing of the hardest thick flows..

The ever-prolific Todd Swain on the first ascent of SHEER ELEGANCE on Mt. Huntington.   Photo by Brad White

Two other climbers, Todd Swain and John Tremblay, though radically different in their approach to ice climbing, also figured prominently during the middle years of the decade.

With all the major areas developed, Swain focused on the obscure, systematically searching out and climbing every bit of ice he could find. During the winter of 1982-83 he was out almost every day his appetite for first ascents sometimes giving him several new routes before dark.

Though few of Swain's climbs were at the top of the difficulty scale, the sheer volume of new routes that he ferreted out of the New England woods has earned him a permanent spot in the region's history.

Tremblay's reputation for devouring ice was legendary as well, although he focused almost exclusively at the highest difficulty. And though his list of first ascents isn't long, the seriousness of some of these routes has diminished little over time. In December of 1986 Tremblay climbed nearly every hard route in New Hampshire (and many elsewhere), many in marginal condition. Later in the season he decided to really test the limits. Thriving on insecurity he put up his most well known route, OVERLOAD, with Dave Rose. This route, on Duck's Head, took over where EAGLE'S GIFT had left off. One hundred feet of vertical verglass with imaginary protection, OVERLOAD barely had enough ice to still be called an ice climb. And with the level of commitment absolute, the need for total control was essential.

Not to be left out of the picture, Lake Willoughby saw perhaps the most activity, at the highest standard. The huge wall that stretches north from the LAST GENTELMAN had always been home to a number of thin runnels that rarely if ever reached the ground. In the early years there had been so many thick flows to climb that no one paid much attention to the skimpy routes. But by the mid 1980's the urge to climb new terrain brought some of New England's best talent to the base of these ephemeral routes. First to fall was the all-ice WHO'S WHO IN OUTER SPACE, a spectacular thin line to the immediate left of THE LAST GENTLEMAN, by Mark Richey and partner in 1984. 1986 saw the addition of two serious and committing mixed routes, AURORA by Ted Hammond and Chris Rowins, and STARMAN by Brad White and Rowins, go up side by side in the same month.

Equally extreme and committing was the practice by a few of linking many hard routes together in a day, often solo. With the latest equipment, the security of climbing vertical ice had been greatly enhanced, and with tremendous energy and confidence, some climbers could get up an almost unfathomable volume of ice in a day. While ten years before it had been quite an accomplishment to solo all the major gullies in Huntington Ravine in a day, people like Randy Rackliff, John Bouchard, Steve Larson, Andy Tuthill and others took the notion a few steps further. The ultimate in this sort of "link-up" may have been Larson and Tuthill's one day ascent of the BLACK DIKE, STANDARD ROUTE at Frankenstein, REPENTENCE, on Cathedral Ledge and PINNACLE GULLY — the latter by headlamp.

John Tremblay on a typical day, this time on the first ascent of WITHOUT REASON, 5+, a free-hanging icicle at Frankenstein.
Photo by S. Peter Lewis

No great leap in difficulty or commitment was seen in the late 1980's and early 1990's. The steepest ice, Lake Willoughby, and the thinnest ice, several Tremblay routes, were now known to be climbable. The fearsom reputation of routes like the BLACK DIKE had mellowed, becoming a pleasant day's outing. Even the somber air of seriousness that had characterized Huntington Ravine a generation before had been replaced with a much more casual confidence, though for the unprepared, unfortunate, or inexperienced few, the ravine continued to be a place of tragedy.

For those with a flair for exploration, this period provided the opportunity to take well-honed skills and climb extreme routes way out in the woods. The sparsely populated hills in western Maine were host to a number of quality routes by climbers like Bob Parrot and Rob Adair and Paul Boissonneault. In the Baker River Valley, Jim Shimberg, Ted Hammond and others found very steep, often thin ice cragging in abundance. Katahdin continued to attract those seeking a committing alpine environment, with a small, dedicated group of climbers leading the exploration. Among the most active were Kevin Slater, Landon Fake, Bob Baribeau, Kurt Winkler, Ben Townsend, and Kevin Codraro.

This period was a time of maturing for New England ice climbing. Most, but certainly not all, of the major routes had now been climbed. And while ice climbing had been viewed as eccentric, it was now established as just one more way to squeeze adventure out of life. There were now many more climbers, and with modern equipment and techniques they began climbing better and faster than ever before. Ten years before, an ascent of REPENTENCE may have been the culmination of a climber's career, now it was not unusual for a climber new to the sport to tick off REPENTENCE early in his career.

A brilliant back-country find, Parrot and Adair's HOT LAVA at Red Rock Mountain.
Photo by Rob Adair

Standing on the shoulders of those who paved the way, ice climbers in the 1990's head out into the mountains with the assurance that almost any ice can be climbed, and they are equiped with the tools to give them the confidence to try. Thus prepared, Willoughby routes like Dave Wright and George Hurley's masterpiece CHINA SHOP and Ted Hammond and Dave Karl's horrendous piller BULLWINKLE are the foundation routes for tomorrow.

The history of climbing has time and time again proven that any definition of "impossible" is temporary at best, and that predicting the future often leads to embarassment. (Remember the remark from *Appalachia* after the first ascent of ODELL'S GULLY that "apparently nothing remained to be done" in Huntington Ravine.) The future of New England ice climbing is anyone's guess. Will there be harder routes? Certainly. Better climbers? Of course. Somewhere there are youngsters that have yet to wear crampons, but who have the ability, determination and vision that will one day make the hardmen of today shake in their boots. In short, the future of ice climbing lies in re-defining the possible, a talent that has characterized human history from the beginning.

S M U G G L E R ' S   N O T C H

Location: Rt. 108 between Stowe and Jeffersonville, VT.

Routes: Grades 1 to 5, wide variety from top rope to desperate.

Access: Park at either end of notch, walk about a mile.

Descent: Bushwhack or rappel.

Weather: *"Notch"*, see pg. 18

Equipment: Standard ice rack, some rock gear.

Highlights: Very secluded, good camping, easy access to many mid-range routes. *Elephant Head Gully, Blind Fate, The Grand Illusion.*

Warning: Rt. 108 is not plowed, heavy snowfall can make approach difficult.

P ▲ TO JEFFERSONVILLE

RT. 108

JEFERSON SLIDE

GRAND ILLUSION — STONE HUT — THE PLAYGROUND

BEAR POND TRAIL

ROCK BUTTRESS

HIDDEN GULLY

CAS'S GULLY ROCK BUTTRESS

ORIGIN OF INTELLIGENCE

ELEPHANT'S HEAD GULLY

BLIND FATE — ELEPHANT'S HEAD

BLUE ICE BULGE — RAGNAROCK

▼ DRIVING FORCE — BLUE ROOM

P ▼ TO STOWE

▲ N

Nestled in the heart of the Green Mountains, Smuggler's Notch is one of the two major centers of ice climbing activity in Vermont. Similar to Frankenstein Cliff in New Hampshire, this scenic notch is lined on either side by climbs from one to four pitches in length encompassing all grades of difficulty. Approaches are usually short and straight forward. Most of the descent routes are the typical New England variety; wade, stumble, or glissade down through the woods on either side of your climb. Occasionally, it will be necessary to rappel down a short cliff band. There are no camping restrictions in the area and several excellent campsites will be found at the top of the notch, especially in boulder caves in the vicinity of the obvious stone hut (an information center in the summer, closed in the winter).

Route 108, which runs through Smuggler's Notch between Stowe and Jefferson, is not maintained in winter. At either end of the plowed road will be a large parking area. The top of the notch is about a mile away from either side and is hiked or skied (sometimes it is possible to hitch a ride on a snowmobile).

Routes in the notch will be described first from south to north on the Mansfield side (west), then back from north to south on the Elephant's Head side (east).

Throughout this guide first ascent information will be catagorized as follows: *FA:* first ascent; *FRA:* first recorded ascent; *FWA:* first winter ascent (for winter ascents of rock climbs only).

DRIVING FORCE I 4
Approaching from Stowe, about halfway up the notch are three climbs on the west side of the road. This is well south of the main climbing area. On the left is a one pitch flow that is moderately steep and on the right is another flow with two steep finishes. DRIVING FORCE climbs the right-hand finish up a very steep column for 50 feet. The left-hand column is also steep but shorter. *FA: Unknown.*

TERROR-TORY II 2-3
A short ice climb to the left of the more readily apparent BLUE ICE BULGE, at the southern end of the notch on the Mansfield side. There is no obvious snow gully leading up to this 150 ft. flow, so bushwhack approximately 300 yds. through the woods from the road to the base. Climb easy ice to a very steep pillar. Climb it directly or bypass it on the left and traverse back right. *FRA: Jeff Lea, Jay Amico, George Seiveright and Roger Hirt, January 12, 1980.*

BLUE ICE BULGE II 2-3
This prominent gully is the left-hand climb of the four prominent routes found on the Mansfield side of the notch. Approach the gully via a long snow slope that leads from the road directly to the base of the four routes. Climb one or two pitches up an obvious flow bordered by a rock wall on the left, and descend off to the right. *FA: Chet Callahan and Dave Cass, Winter 1969-70.*

NORTON GIBNEY II 4
To the right of BLUE ICE BULGE, work up icy slabs and over bulges until a belay stance to the right of the final column is reached. Climb the steep pillar, and continue past several more bulges until the angle lays back. Descend as for the previous climb. *FA: Dave Norton and Frank Gibney, Winter 1974-75.*

BLIND FATE III 4

This is the next flow to the right. Two pitches and two columns characterize this sustained line. The latter steep section is some thirty feet high. Two rappels or the woods on the right offer a means of descent.
FA: John Bouchard and Rick Wilcox, Winter 1974-75.

BLIND FAITH II 3

Little is known about the nature of this route. It ascends an iced-up corner which is slightly to the right of the former climb.
FA: Bob Olsen, Chuck Bond and Alan Long, Winter 1971-72.

CASS'S GULLY II 1

To the right of BLIND FAITH is a large tree-covered buttress. The gully on its right-hand side is CASS'S GULLY. It is easily seen from the road from the top of the notch. The gully is typically full of snow, but there could be a little ice mixed in. Pass by a large chockstone at the top of the gully to where the angle eases, then descend via rappel down the tree-covered buttress.
FA: Dave Cass, Winter 1968-69.

HIDDEN GULLY I 2-3

The route is only visible to the west several hundred yards south of the top of the notch. Approach the gully once it comes into view. The initial portion is quite narrow. Climb past a few ice bulges to the first snowfield. Continue to the next larger snowfield and either descend EASY GULLY on the right, or finish up any of the three more difficult finishes. From left to right they become progressively easier. Each one is 1-2 pitches in length.
FA: Dave Cass and Phil Koch climbed up to the second snowfield and presumably descended EASY GULLY. John Bouchard soloed the hardest finish in the winter of 1973-74.

EASY GULLY I 1

Around the corner to the right is an easy snow-filled gully leading up to the second snowfield on HIDDEN GULLY. A rock barrier separates the two gullies. Most climbers use EASY GULLY as a means of descent from the middle of HIDDEN GULLY, or as a very easy snow climb. A rappel is necessary to enter the gully from above.
FA: Unknown.

THE GRAND ILLUSION III 4 +

Located to the right of EASY GULLY, but above the point where the Bear

Steve Zajchowski starts up the NORTON GIBNEY route, an early climb at Smuggler's that finishes with an impressive column.

Photo by Peter Cole

Pond Trail comes down through the woods. A classic hard route.
FA: John Bouchard and Steve Zajchowski, February, 1975.

GRAND CONFUSION I 3+
Named because it is commonly mistaken for GRAND ILLUSION, it lies to the north of that route. Approach up the slide path directly behind the stone hut (about 450 feet). Head up and left to the base of this one pitch route. Highly recommended.
FA: Unknown.

ENT GULLY II 2
Approach the route from the bend in the road north of the parking lot at the crest. The climb, a two-pitch low-angled gully with large rock walls on both sides, is not visible from the road. Rappel the route.
FA: Todd Swain, Chris Taylor, Don MacDougal and Ned Getchell, Winter 1980.

JEFFERSON SLIDE I 2-4
About 250 yards north of the stone hut, at the first sharp left-hand turn, head into the woods on the left. Walk across a small plateau and then down a steep hill (keeping right) to the bottom of the slide. The slide is about 200 feet wide and a pitch and a half tall with many lines possible from grade 2 to 4.
FA: Unknown.

Routes will now be descibed north to suth on the east (left) side of the road.

WORKOUT WALL I 3-4
Approximately 3/4 of a mile up from the Jeffersonville side on Route 108 there is a cluster of short columns about fifty feet off the road on the left. This area offers quick access and good top roping.
FA: Unknown.

THE PLAYGROUND I 3-4
Found on the Elephant's Head side of the notch at the so-called "top of the Notch," the PLAYGROUND is a very popular practice area, even though most of the routes are fairly difficult. A steep open slope below the ice flows is the best approach. Most of the flows are about 50 feet high. The routes are easily top-roped .
FA: Unknown.

ORIGIN OF INTELLIGENCE IN CHILDREN III 4+
Just north of Elephant's Head are two steep ice flows. This is the left-hand flow. Two short pitches up a series of tiers.
FA: Steve Zajchowski and John Bouchard, Winter 1974-75.

WATERSHIP DOWN III 4+
Climb the narrow, sustained right-hand ice ribbon. One or two pitches.
FA: Steve Zajchowski and John Bouchard, Winter 1974-75.

ELEPHANT'S HEAD GULLY II 3
The gully to the left of this noticeable landmark. The route is quite easy except for one section of roughly ten feet, and is typically done in two or three pitches. Descend to the left of ORIGIN OF INTELLIGENCE IN CHILDREN, or walk around either end of the cliff to get down.
FA: Chet Callahan, Bob Olsen and Chuck Bond, Winter 1969-70.

ELEPHANT'S HEAD, THE SOUTH FACE II 4
A difficult mixed route. Begin at the right-hand corner of the rock, then climb up into a dihedral. Mixed climbing leads to the top.
FA: John Bouchard, Winter 1973-74.

THE CREIGHTON-KORMAN ROUTE III 5
To the right of the former route and left of RAGNAROCK climb the buttress for three pitches, the first one mixed.
FA: Geoff Creighton and Josh Korman, January, 1985.

RAGNAROCK III 4 +
One of the Notch's early difficult routes. One hundred feet or more south of Elephant's Head on a smaller section of the same cliff is a massive ice flow. Depending on conditions and your choice of starts, RAGNAROCK is a three pitch ice climb. Conditions and stability vary considerably.
FA: John Bouchard and Steve Zajchowski, Winter 1974-75.

HAVE A CIGAR I 4+
The prominent pillar south of RAGNAROCK, and left of BLUE ROOM.
FA: Unknown.

BLUE ROOM II 3+
A massive flow to the right of RAGNAROCK. Three pitches.
FA: Unknown.

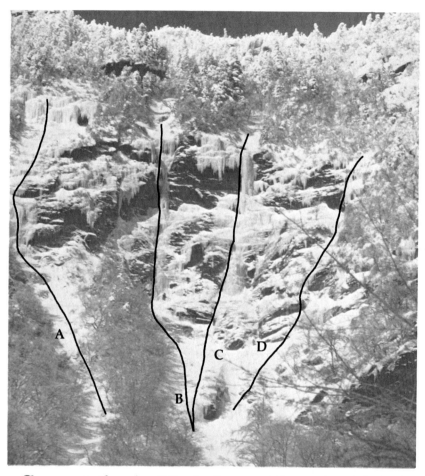

Smuggler's Notch — North Side

Elephant's Head

LAKE WILLOUGHBY

Location: Rt. 5, 8 miles north of Lyndonville, VT.

Routes: Grades 3-5, most routes are upper grade and long.

Access: Park below route, 15 minute to 1/2 hour approach.

Descent: Rappel or use descent trail around south end of cliff.

Weather: *"Notch"* sunny but can be very windy and cold. See pg. 18

Equipment: Large standard ice rack, double ropes.

Highlights: An incredible volume of ice. Up to five pitches of near vertical ice climbing. *Last Gentleman, Called on Account of Rains, Mindbender.*

Lake Willoughby to the north of West Burke, Vermont, is one of the most dramatic ice climbing areas in New England. The massive ice flows decorating the precipitous west face of Mount Pisgah are unrivalled in sheer size, verticality, and sustained difficulty. There is more steep ice here than at any other area in New England. Ice climbs here are substantial undertakings with no routes easier than grade 3. In addition, its remote location dictates the need for safe and responsible climbing.

To approach Lake Willoughby from the south, drive north on Interstate 91 to Route 5 and follow this to Lyndonville. North of Lyndonville, branch right on Route 5A in West Burke and drive another seven miles to the lake. Park at any of several plowed pull-outs along the road beneath Mount Pisgah. The drive takes 5 hours from Boston and 2 hours from North Conway in ideal conditions, an hour longer if the roads are icy. Several factors—ease of access and descent, and generally thick and reliable ice—have stimulated a tremendous increase in popularity in the area in recent years.

While the climbs do receive afternoon sun, the wind chill factor can be extreme at Lake Willoughby so dress accordingly. The approaches to the climbs take about thirty minutes and are straightforward in good conditions; simply walk straight up to your route from below. Bear in mind however, that the approach slopes can vary from hard ice that requires the use of crampons, to deep snow that could avalanche. Don't hesitate to rope up on the approach if conditions warrant it. A hiking trail follows the cliff's edge from the south end up to the top of THE LAST GENTLEMAN, after which it turns uphill to the summit of Mount Pisgah. For all routes south of RENORMALIZATION you will usually find a climber's packed trail that skirts the edge of the cliff connecting with the main trail above THE LAST GENTLEMAN. To reach the parking lot, leave the trail near the bottom and descend a short gully on the right, either downclimbing or sometimes rappelling if conditions are dangerous. If climbing on the trio of routes at the north end of the cliff, one long rappel with two ropes from the top of RENORMALIZATION will get you to the base, and another short rappel from a tree will get you to walking terrain.

Deep snow or poor weather can make Willoughby's relatively easy descents treacherous so be on the lookout for rappel anchors as you climb and don't hesitate to bail out if things don't go according to plan. Routes will now be described north to south.

PLUG AND CHUG II 5
The farthest left ice flow on the west face of Mount Pisgah, and the left-hand of a group of three ice climbs. A two-pitch ice route, not as serious as its neighbor, MINDBENDER, but strenuous enough. Don't run out of energy on the crux. Descend left or rappel as described above.
FA: Clint Cummins, Brinton Young and John Imbrie, February 20, 1977.

MINDBENDER III 5+
The central ice flow, steep and unrelenting. A two-pitch route which has a notoriously sustained vertical pillar on the first pitch and additional hardships higher up. Descend left or rappel as described above.
FA: Clint Cummins and John Imbrie, February 13, 1977.

RENORMALIZATION I 4
The right-hand flow of the trio and the most reasonable route of the three. Its close proximity to the road, shorter length, and less severe technical difficulties make it a popular route.
FA: John Imbrie and Nancy Kerrebrock, February 20, 1977.

Steve Larson on MINDBENDER's incredible pillar, one of the longest, steepest stretches of ice at Lake Willoughby.

Photo by Paul Boissonneault

SHAKER HEIGHTS III 4 (alternate finishes 5, 4+ 5.7)

Situated immediately left of the northern end of the main rock face of Mount Pisgah, this route offers an alternative to the typically arm-destroying routes found at Lake Willoughby. A highly recommended route with generally moderate bulges and three or four pitches of climbing. The route can be done all the way to the top of the cliff but this does involve harder climbing. The left finish is up steep ice (4+) and then some 5.7 mixed climbing while the right-hand finish climbs a grade 5 ice column over an overhang. From the top of the cliff, descend up and then right linking with the trail from the top of THE LAST GENTLEMAN. If you choose not to do either direct finish, then rappel the route from trees.
FA: Ken Andrasko and Chris Field, Winter 1974-75. Direct finishes: Unknown.

VARIATION: LEDGE APPROACH III 4

Beginning Just to the right of SHAKER HEIGHTS, gain a fairly obvious ledge system which leads right to the upper ice on CALLED ON ACCOUNT OF RAINS. Two or three ice pitches lead to the top. To descend, rappel l50 ft. from trees to the left end of the ledge system, then to the ground.
FA: John Imbrie and Clint Cummins, February 19, 1976.

CALLED ON ACCOUNT OF RAINS IV 5

A very impressive mixed route, the left-hand of a group of ice flows that rarely, if ever, reaches the ground. Very dicey mixed rock and ice climbing gains the base of the ice flow, which is followed to the top in another four pitches. A variety of pitons and nuts should be carried to protect the initial pitch.
FA: Clint Cummins and John Imbrie, December 28, 1977.

AURORA IV 4+ 5.8 A2

This route and its neighbor STARMAN climb the central wall left of BRINTON'S FOLLY crossing at mid height. Begin left of STARMAN at a gully/depression; climb up and right and then up rock (5.8 A2) to reach a terrace above and the junction with STARMAN. Pitches 2-4 go up grade 4 ice to the right of the final pitches of STARMAN. Pitch 5 goes up and right surmounting an overhang at a fixed knifeblade and then to the top.
FA: Ted Hammond and Chris Rowins, February, 1986.

STARMAN IV 5+ 5.8

Begin at a buttress near a large flake; climb up a chimney past a chockstone to a small snow field. Then go up the next tier to a belay at trees. Continue up a corner and easy ground to a major ledge system at mid-height on the face. Go left for a full pitch, crossing AURORA to reach the middle of three parallel flows at the top of the cliff. Up this for three more pitches of steep ice and hard mixed ground to the top.

An alternate start avoids the lower mixed pitches by going up an easy gully farther right (the approach gully for BRINTON'S FOLLY) and traversing left to join the route where it crosses AURORA.

FA: Brad White and Chris Rowins, February 15, 1986.

BRINTON'S FOLLY I 4

To the south of the previous climb is a large open snowfield below a right facing gully, running diagonally up to a narrow terrace. This climb is the short ice fall above the approach gully. It does not go to the top of the cliff. After one pitch of steep ice, rappel off from trees with two ropes.

FA: John Imbrie and Brinton Young, February 21, 1977.

STORMY MONDAY III 4 +

Use the same approach as BRINTON'S FOLLY to reach the terrace, then traverse right to the base of a long, narrow ice flow. Three difficult pitches, involving thin ice in places, lead to the top. Rappel off trees down the northern border of the route to reach the terrace.

FA: Rainsford Rouner and Gustavo Brillembourg, February 12, 1977.

CHINA SHOP IV 5+

Midway between Stormy Monday and Who's Who in Outer Space climb a narrow runnel of ice in an inside corner or gain a traverse ledge from the right and belay below a thicker ice flow. Five pitches of steep ice with the crux column on the fourth lead gain the top. The crux column is rarely in shape.

FA: Dave Wright and George Hurley, January 18, 1991.

WHO'S WHO IN OUTER SPACE IV 5

This spectacular route climbs the flow immediately left of THE LAST GENLELMAN. The first pitch is usually the crux and climbs near-vertical ice normally just a couple of inches thick for a hundred feet. Above, follow thicker ice for two to three more pitches to the top.

FA: Mark Richey and Neil Pothier, January, 1984.

THE LAST GENTLEMAN IV 5

This route ascends the left-hand of two immense ice falls in an amphitheater near the center of the west face of Mount Pisgah. Length, beauty, and an awesome amount of steep ice make this route one of the classic ice routes in

New England. The climb is commonly done in either four or five pitches, depending on whether the direct start is in shape; it usually isn't. Most ascents begin by ascending the first pitch of THE PROMENADE to the top of an ice column (bolt). Now traverse left on moderate mixed ground to the main flow. Overcome a difficult vertical section (the crux) past a cave. Two more very difficult pitches lead to the woods, with the usual finish up the right-hand column. Bring some blade pitons for the rock traverse.
FA: Rainsford and Tim Rouner over several days. December, 1976.

THE PROMENADE IV 5 +

One of the most difficult and demanding ice climbs in the region. Long vertical sections, hollow ice, and free-standing columns call for superior techniques and a mastery of the sport. The crux ice column takes a while to come into shape. Begin by climbing the initial ice flow to a ledge at its top, then continue up a difficult hollow sheet of ice to a cave belay. This pitch may be split. Above, persevere up a vertical free-standing column to easier ground. One final steep flow, with some stemming possible, leads to the woods.
FA: Tim and Rainsford Rouner and Peter Cole, over two days in January, 1977.

REIGN OF TERROR III 5

Ascends the steep ice flow on the right-hand side of the amphitheater where THE LAST GENTLEMAN and THE PROMENADE are located. Approach the amphitheater by way of an open avalanche scar from the roadside. Begin with about one hundred feet of relatively low angle ice which is followed to the base of a thin, steep runnel. Belay at its top up on the right off a tree. An alternate approach (the original first pitch is very rarely in shape) is possible by moving up and left from the top of the first pitch of BULLWINKLE. Above, climb the very sustained vertical tower to the forest. As of this writing, no second ascent has been confirmed. Descend as for the LAST GENTLEMAN up through the woods to a trail and then down to the right.
FA: Matt Peer and Tom Dickey, January 17, 1981.

BULLWINKLE III 5+

In terms of sheer verticality, this route epitomizes ice climbing at Lake Willoughby, ascending an unrelentingly steep free-standing icicle. Start to the right of REIGN OF TERROR at a bulge. Either climb the bulge directly or walk up and around on the left. Continue up moderate terrain to a belay below the obvious, mushroomed, icicle. Then just tighten your wrist loops and go for it!
FA: Ted Hammond and Dave Karl, January 27, 1984.

Gerry Handren and Mike Brown in a sea of vertical ice on THE LAST GENTLEMAN, one of Lake Willoughby's classic hard routes.

Photo by Peter Hovling

FLOAT LIKE A BUTTERFLY (LAND LIKE A TOMATO) II 4+

The often thin ice flow just left of TWENTY BELOW ZERO GULLY. Climb diagonally left to reach typically thin and unprotected ice. Above, the flow gets thicker and steeper. Three pitches.

FA: Bryan Becker, Peter Cole and Tad Pheffer, December 25, 1976.

TWENTY BELOW ZERO GULLY III 4+

One of the first routes to be climbed at Lake Willoughby. The route is anything but a gully! Very popular. Take the line of least resistance for two pitches to a cave belay which protects the belayer from falling ice while the leader attacks the final and steepest section.

FA: Henry Barber, Michael Hartrich and Al Rubin, January, 1974.

GLASS MENAGERIE III 5

Located on the ice covered wall between TWENTY BELOW ZERO GULLY and EXTENSIVE HOMOLOGY. Delicacy combined with bravado is the preferred technique on this steep route, which is usually done in three pitches. Although the start is long and sustained, the top column is the crux.

FA: Tim Rouner and Chip Lee, February 18, 1977.

EXTENSIVE HOMOLOGY III 5

A formidable route, the last to be climbed on this section of the cliff. The first pitch is often non-existent, but occasionally boasts thinly iced slabs and poor protection. The finish is also horrendous (i.e., unrelentingly steep).

FA: John Imbrie and Dennis Drayna, January 31, 1979.

VARIATION: UN-NAMED II 4+ 5.9

To the right of the former route is yet another steep column at the top of the cliff. Though not as difficult as its neighbors the route makes up for it by offering a thin start and a few hard rock moves to gain the upper ice. If you don't like the looks of this, a traverse in from the midpoint of routes to the left is a reasonable way to reach the top column.

FA: Unknown.

CRAZY DIAMOND III 4+

The first major ice flow to the left of the three TABLETS and just left of ZEPHYR. Climb moderate ice over bulges to a belay at the base of the upper vertical columns. Climb these energetically, stemming to reduce the pump factor, to the finish and the woods.

FA: John Imbrie and Clint Cummins, December 2, 1977.

ZEPHYR II 3 5.4

The flow between CRAZY DIAMOND and the TABLET LEFT. Up the ice for a full pitch to a belay at trees. Move right to the buttress and up that to the top. Descend down the trail or rappel with two ropes.

FA: Todd Swain and Ray Dobkin, March 5, 1983.

THE TABLETS

In previous climbing guides these flows on the south end of Mt. Pisgah have gone by the unfortunate designation of the PRACTICE SLABS. Though these climbs pale in comparison with the likes of the LAST GENTLEMAN and other routes to the immediate north, if they were found alone any place else they would undoubtedly become destinations in themselves. And with grades up to solid 4, perhaps a little practice before attempting them would be prudent. In an effort to give these wonderful climbs some of the dignity they deserve, the local designation for the area, THE TABLETS, will be used here.

TABLET LEFT II 4

The left most of the three slabs is the most difficult. Two pitches of steep ice lead to the forest.

FA: Unknown.

TABLET CENTER I 3 +

One of the two easiest ice climbs at Lake Willoughby. Both the center and right TABLETS offer the easiest ice climbs at Lake Willoughby. They are quite popular as a result. Two pitches.

FA: Unknown.

TABLET RIGHT I 3

The easiest of the three slabs, it is two pitches in length. Wander up the flow over a variety of ice bulges to the top.

FA: Unknown.

Mount Pisgah — North

A.	PLUG AND CHUG	5	55
B.	MINDBENDER	5+	55
C.	RENORMALIZATION	4	55

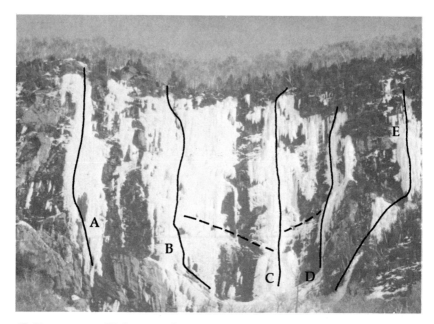

Mount Pisgah — Last Gentleman Area

A.	WHO'S WHO IN OUTER SPACE	5	58
B.	THE LAST GENTLEMAN (Promenade start dashed)	5	58
C.	THE PROMENADE	5+	59
D.	REIGN OF TERROR (Promenade start dashed)	5	59
E.	BULLWINKLE	5+	59

Mount Pisgah — South

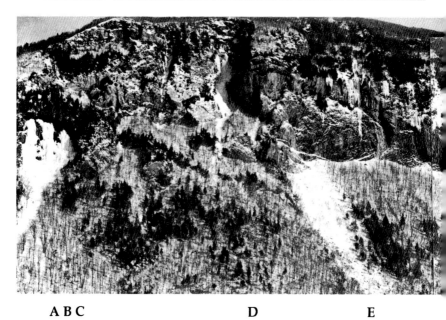

 A B C   D   E

Mou

A.	PLUG AND CHUG	5		55
B.	MINDBENDER	5+		55
C.	RENORMALIZATION	4		55
D.	SHAKER HEIGHTS	4-5	5.7	57
E.	CALLED ON ACCOUNT OF RAINS	5+		57
F.	AURORA	4+	5.8 A2	57
G.	STARMAN	5+	5.8	57

F G   H   I J K   L   M

sgah

MOUNT HOR

Across Lake Willoughby from Mount Pisgah, stands Mt. Hor. If you're intimidated by the vertical ice of Pisgah the low angled ice slabs on this mountain may offer a suitable alternative. The following route is a good possibility.

WOOBER GOOBER GULLY II 3 +.

On the road, a quarter mile south of Lake Willoughby, look to the left and you'll see a snow and ice gully running up the south side of Mt. Hor. Approach across the lake and up through the woods to the southern end of the face. After a short and steep first pitch, climb over moderate ice bulges on the second lead until one last pitch leads to the gully's end. Traverse left forty feet, then finish up thinly iced slabs. Descend down and left through the forest.

FRA: Wayne Domeier, Gene Popien and Tom Nonis, February 15, 1981. Henry Barber and Al Rubin did a route here in 1974 that may have followed the same basic line. Their ascent was before the first ascent of TWENTY BELOW ZERO GULLY and their comment was that "it was very hard when we did it." Considering the gear available at the time, it must have been desperate.

THE BOISSONNEAULT-CATTABRIGA ROUTE I 4

Several hundred yards north of WOOBER GOOBER is an obvious cliff band which diagonals up and left. Just past the bottom of this is a distinct short column.

FA: Paul Boissonneault and Alan Cattabriga, February, 1991.

In addition to these routes, there are other possibilities on Mount Hor including a steep route by Kurt Winkler between WOOBER GOOBER GULLY and THE BOISSONNEAULT-CATTABRIGA ROUTE. Information regarding other activity in the area has been hard to verify.

CRYSTAL LAKE

Crystal Lake is a small lake located a few miles due west of Lake Willoughby and is reached by bearing left onto Route 5 in West Burke and going north for twelve miles. The climbs are located on the far side of Crystal Lake on a short cliff band and are easily visible from the road. The ice flows which form here are generally much shorter and more mellow than those on Mount Pisgah. The main icefall is grade 3. A more difficult pillar lies to the left.

JOB'S POND

Job's Pond is located east of Lake Willoughby and is reached by turning right in West Burke just north of the junction of Routes 5 and 5A and driving about nine miles to the pond.

JOB'S PILLAR II 4

Park at the pond and walk across if well frozen. This two pitch route will be very obvious on the far side.

FRA: Chris Ellms and Mike Brochu, early 1980's.

FRANCONIA NOTCH

Location: Rt. 93, ten miles north of Lincoln, NH.

Routes: Grades 4 and up, serious.

Access: Park at base, one hour approach.

Descent: Walk off either end, long.

Weather: *"Notch"* windy, cold, see page 18.

Equipment: Standard rack plus lots of rock gear, double ropes.

Highlights: Home of super-classic *Black Dike*, also long mixed routes like *Fafnir, Omega, Whitney Gilman Ridge.*

Warning: Registration at Profile Lake, very serious alpine terrain, be prepared for anything.

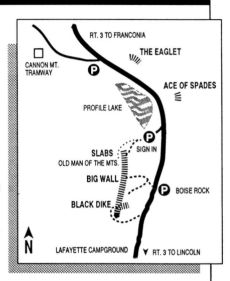

Desolate in winter, with the wind often howling through the valley, Franconia Notch is the scene of some of the most serious alpine ice routes in New England. Highly technical difficulties, sub-zero temperatures, and hazardous access and retreat make ice climbs on Cannon Cliff very committing. During the short winter days, one must always be on the move to avoid becoming benighted. Wading through waist deep powder snow for a mile or two can be harder than the climb itself. Winter routes on Cannon are for experienced climbers only.

Construction in the late 1980's has restricted traffic flow through the notch making east exits possible only when heading north and west exits possible only when heading south. You can reverse directions at exit 2 at the Tramway (when heading north) and at exit 1, 4 1/2 miles south of the Tramway (when heading south). The two traditional climber parking areas, Boise rock, reached northbound only, and Profile Lake, reached via a southbound exit only, are still available with no restrictions. Boise Rock makes for a shorter approach to the

Big Wall section of the cliff and the Black Dike, while Profile Lake is closer to the north end of the cliff. For routes on the east side of the notch, park at Profile Lake.

To approach Cannon Cliff in winter from Boise Rock, cross the stream next to Route 3 via the small wooden footbridge. Walk north on a trail running parallel to the stream for about a 100 yards until a narrow climber's trail diverges to the left. This can be hard to locate if there has been a heavy snowfall. After crossing a paved bicycle path, continue to follow the narrow climber's trail to the talus slope and make your way to the base of the cliff. During heavy snow years and under the right conditions, the snow slopes on the scree pile have been known to avalanche, so ascend carefully. From Profile Lake follow a trail from the south end of the lake and then a faint climber's path on the right to reach the talus. Don't count on either the approach or descent trails being packed out. An unmaintained trail runs along the top of the entire cliff and descends around either end. It can be hard or impossible to follow after a storm.

Probably the most important action to take when climbing in Franconia Notch is to sign out and in at a box located at the south end of Profile Lake, stating your proposed climb and descent. Do not forget to sign in after the climb! This check-in system is taken very seriously and if you appear to be overdue, rescue will be initiated. There is no longer a sign-in box at Boise Rock, so if you plan to park here it is imperative that you sign in and out at Profile Lake.

The major winter routes in Franconia Notch are located on Cannon Cliff. A popular top-roping area at The Flume, located on the east side of the notch six miles south of Cannon Cliff, will be described first, then the main routes on Cannon from south to north, and finally the remaining climbs located immediately to the south of The Eaglet, a free-standing pinnacle at the top of the notch on the east side.

Winter ascents of summer rock routes are noted for historical value only. Accurate route descriptions can be found in the rock climbing guides to the area. First winter ascents of rock climbs are described with the initials *FWA*. Ice conditions vary so much that in some years crampons are necessary for the ascents, while in other years only rock shoes will be required. An ice grade may be listed for them if or when they can be done under normal or ideal winter ice conditions.

THE FLUME

THE FLUME I 3+-5

Located about six miles south of Cannon Mt., this spectacular gorge is a great sheltered place to top rope some very steep ice. A very handy alternative if you get to Cannon and find the weather conditions on the face attrocious. Five miles north of Lincoln on Route 3, signs will lead you to the proper exit for The Flume. Park in the lot and follow a trail for about a half mile to the gorge. A walkway leads through the center of The Flume, a deep gorge bordered by steep rock walls. The right-hand wall is usually covered with hard ice varying from verglass to thick flows. All the routes will be steep and anchors are easily found on top. Descend around either end or rappel.

Also in the vicinity is "the Pool" a huge pot hole in the Pemigewasset River that is home to a unique climb. Signs at The Flume visitor center will direct you to the proper trail. Directly over the water is a bright yellow free-standing column (rated 4+). Rapell to the base and lead, or top rope this spectacular formation.
FA: Todd Swain, solo, early 1980's.

CANNON CLIFF

LA DEEPFREEZE II 2-3

A short route located about 300 feet left of OMEGA, on the south side of the Henderson Buttress. Ascend a very easy 200 foot gully to a tree ledge. Continue on hard mixed ground or rappel off.
FA: Todd Swain and Brad White, January 17, 1981.

HENDERSON II 5.5

A snow-packed rock climb.
FWA: Ajax Greene and Rick Mulhern, 1974.

OMEGA IV 5 +

An extreme route which epitomizes the desperate nature of modern ice climbs with its thinly-verglassed start, mixed climbing, and steep final columns. A classic of the region which rarely comes into shape. The route ascends the prominent icefall on the southern end of Cannon Cliff. A couple of hundred yards south of the WHITNEY GILMAN RIDGE, past an obvious short buttress, is another rather vague buttress with a shallow amphitheater at its base. Hard mixed climbing. Rock gear (including pins) is recommended.

Begining on a verglass covered slab, mixed climbing leads to a belay near the base of the thicker flow coming down from above. Climb the upper flow for three more pitches, weaving up through overhangs on steep yellow columns. The crux is typically a sustained pillar a pitch below the top.

The exact nature of this route varies considerably from year to year, and the best line and belay points depend on conditions.

FA: John Bouchard and Rainsford Rouner, February, 1976.

THE WHITNEY-GILMAN RIDGE II 5.7

One of the best winter routes on Cannon, with superb mixed climbing and exposed situations. Highly recommended.

FWA: Leif Patterson and Henry W. Kendall, 1962.

ACROSS THE GREAT DIVIDE IV 5.7 A4

Climbs the somber wall to the left of THE BLACK DIKE. The first ascent of this difficult climb was done over several days in full winter conditions.

FA: Peter Cole and Rick Wilcox climbed the first pitch; Cole, Mark Richey and Rainsford Rouner did the second; and Cole and Wilcox finished the climb in November, 1975.

THE BLACK DIKE IV 5-

Since its first ascent, THE BLACK DIKE has become a measuring stick for many aspiring ice climbers. Its length, sustained but not extreme technical difficulties, and tremendous atmosphere make it one of the most alpine of ice routes in New England. In poor conditions, below zero temperatures and spindrift flowing, the route takes on a whole other character of seriousness. Be prepared physically and mentally for the climb.

John Bouchard soloed the first ascent on December 18, 1971, in sub-zero temperatures in a snow storm. His account of the epic ascent (described in the History chapter) was doubted by many at the time. Because he was just a teenager with relatively little experience, the locals were reluctant to buy his claim to New England's biggest plum. Bouchard returned the following winter and climbed the route with Rick Wilcox, Henry Barber, and John Bragg. Fixed gear high on the route, which matched Bouchard's description, cleared up the mystery of his solo ascent and restored his honor.

Ray Omerza works his way up the the lower section of THE BLACK DIKE. An uncomprimising line in a spectacular alpine setting, THE BLACK DIKE combines hard ice, difficult rock and harsh weather to create what many feel is the classic alpine route in New England.

Photo by S. Peter Lewis

Hike up to the base of the Whitney-Gilman Ridge; THE BLACK DIKE is the immense gully on the north side of the ridge. Work up low-angled snow and ice, then trend right over bulges until reaching a belay stance below a pronounced rock wall. Climb the notorious rock traverse moving back left into the main inside corner. At rare times there is a narrow runnel of ice leading straight up to the main inside corner, making it possible to avoid the rock traverse. Fifty feet of this steep inside corner brings the climber to lower angle ice. Rock belay on the left. The next pitch is easier and climbs more bulges to one of several stances. Follow the ice on the left to the very top of the dike, or exit lower to the right into the woods. Hike uphill until intersecting the descent trail which leads down around the left end of the cliff. This trail can be difficult to follow in winter. Be careful to stay back away from the main cliff and head south until the cliff is safely passed, then down to the highway .
FA: *John Bouchard, December 18, 1971.*

VARIATION (HASSIG'S DIRECT) 5
Climb mixed rock and ice directly above the first belay on THE BLACK DIKE instead of the usual traverse to the ice ribbon.
FA: *Chris Hassig, February, 1979.*

FAFNIR IV 5
Descending in a series of steps on the right, this is the sister ice flow of THE BLACK DIKE. The difficult mixed climbing at the top is the crux. Wait for thick enough conditions. Climb the first two pitches, or one very long pitch, of THE BLACK DIKE to the right of the rock traverse. Belay on the right on a narrow, snow covered ledge at the base of the main flow. Step right, then climb a series of vertical steps to a good belay platform at the base of the final mixed portion. Take the line of least resistance straight up following a fairly obvious weakness, stepping off right at the top. The last pitch varies from bare rock to thick ice bulges.
FA: *John Bouchard, Steve Zajchowski and Roger Martin, December ,1975.*

LILA IV 4+ A2
Ascends the thinly iced slab to the right of FAFNIR, then the improbable upper headwall. The route requires good conditions to form, and even at that, aid is necessary on the last pitch. Carry rock pegs, etriers, etc. Climb the verglassed slab to the left of the Cannonade Buttress for two pitches. Follow the ice as high as possible up steep ground and use small amounts of aid to reach easier mixed climbing above.
FA: *Rainsford Rouner and Nancy Kerrebrock, March,1976.*

Another Cannon classic, FAFNIR climbs the wall right of THE BLACK DIKE via a series of steep yellow ice smears connected by hard mixed climbing up blocky walls. Here Tom Nonis and Wayne Domeier begin the final pitch.

Photo by S. Peter Lewis

CANNONADE II 2-3 5.4
Mixed climbing on nebulous terrain. Not a popular winter climb.
FWA: Robert Hall, Jorge Uriosite and Joe Boden, 1967.

QUARTET ICE HOSE IV 4+ 5.8, A2
A difficult mixed climb which ascends the ice runnel in the back of Quartet Corner to the upper slabs of the Hanson-Echardt Memorial. Carry a large variety of gear.
Ed Webster and Todd Swain made a nearly complete ascent in January, 1981, retreating from near the top in the dark in very cold weather. The first two leads had been climbed earlier by Peter Cole. On December 9-10, 1989, Chris Dube and Larry Sodano made the first complete ascent in full winter conditions.

DUET III 5.7
A rapid, six hour ascent in snowy conditions.
FWA: Andy Tuthill and Chris Ellms in 1977.

ICARUS IV 5.8, A4
The first new route to be climbed on Cannon in winter (by the calendar). One bivouac was made on the face. John Bouchard completed the route despite the fact that he broke his ankle in a fall near the top.
FA: John Bouchard and Rick Wilcox, with help from Jeff Pheasant, January, 1974.

SAM'S SWAN SONG III 5.7
A very impressive winter ascent considering the year. Hard mixed terrain.
FWA: Robert Proudman and Mark Lawrence over two days in 1967.

THE GHOST IV 5.7, A3
This arduous big wall climb also received its first winter ascent at an early date. A large ice flow was climbed to the top.
FWA: John Bouchard, Rick Wilcox and Henry Barber climbed the route over two days in 1973.

VMC DIRECT DIRECT IV 5.10 (5.7, A2)
A tour-de-force which took four days and one bivouac in hammocks on the face.
FWA: John Bouchard, Jeff Pheasant, David Belden (France) and Jean-Claude Droyer (France) in 1975.

LABIRYNTH WALL V 5.7, A4

Rainsford Rouner and Peter Cole made the first winter ascent in warm weather in February, 1976. John Bouchard and Andy Embick followed a day later in worse conditions. Both ascents included a bivouac.

FA: John Bouchard and Andy Embick, February, 1976.

FRUIT CUP WALL V 5.8, A4

Another Wall route that will feature hard aid and some mixed ground. The first winter ascent was done in moderate conditions. One bivouac was made on the face.

FWA: Mark Richey soloed all but the last pitch in 1975 (while still in high school!). Mark Whiton, Bryan Becker and Alain Comeau climbed the first complete ascent in1978.

MOBY GRAPE III 5.8

A superb free-climb done in rapid time; mostly rock climbing.

FWA: Andy Tuthill and Chris Ellms in February, 1976.

UNION JACK III 5.9

Yet another cold rock climb following the summer route to the right of the Conn Buttress.

FWA: Chris Hassig and friend in 1978.

VERTIGO III 5.9

A commendable two-day ascent. The climbers used nuts for protection and they used very little direct aid.

FWA: Chris Hassig and Dave Foster in 1976.

NORTH-SOUTH-WEST III 5.8-9

A confusing enough route in summer without the added difficulties of snow and ice.

FWA: Chris Ellms and Andy Tuthill in 1976.

UNKNOWN

An ice climb which leads from the base of Wiessner's Buttress to the Old Cannon Garden. Seldom in shape.

FA: Andy Tuthill and Jim Rossin, 1976.

OLD CANNON II 5.6

A true winter winter adventure, provided conditions are good, with a 300

foot ice slab at the top. The first winter ascent took four days of climbing time.
FWA: Robert Hall and Jorge Uriosite in 1971.

WIESSNER'S BUTTRESS II 5.6
 A long and worthwhile mixed route.
FWA: Joe Cote and Steve Arsenault in 1971.

LAKEVIEW II 2 5.5
 The slabs were entirely coated in water ice and snow.
FWA: Tom Lyman, Rick Wilcox and A.J. LaFleur, Winter 1969.

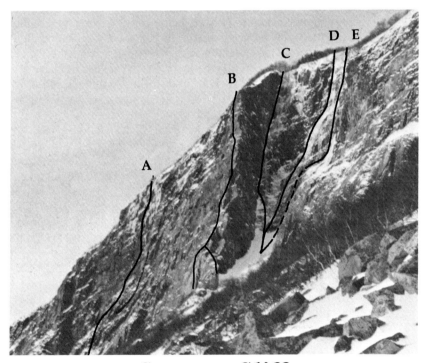

Cannon Cliff

A.	OMEGA	5+		72
B.	THE WHITNEY GILMAN RIDGE	—	5.7	73
C.	THE BLACK DIKE	5-		73
D.	FAFNIR	5		75
E.	LILA	4+	A2	75

THE EAGLET

The following ice routes are located on the cliffs to the south of the Eaglet, the rock pinnacle across Route 3 from the Old Man Parking Lot and the Tramway Station. The approach to all climbs is a desperate bushwack of about a half mile uphill. Snowshoes are sometimes necessary. Routes are described north to south.

GARCIA-VEGA III 4

This route follows the ice flow in a left-facing corner to the south of the Eaglet and a narrow scree gully. Approach as for the Eaglet across the highway from the parking lot. Once at the base of the climb, ascend thin ice up an increasingly steep face, the crux. Belay just to the left of the dihedral itself. Traverse right into a chimney on the second pitch, pass over a chockstone and finish up slabs leading into the woods. To descend, first head up and left, then back down the same scree gully mentioned previously.

FA: Rainsford Rouner, Michael Hartrich and Peter Cole in January, 1975.

The next three routes are found to the south of GARCIA-VEGA and just to the north of ACE OF SPADES. Approach as for ACE OF SPADES.

SHORT TRICK II 3

About 200 feet left of ACE OF SPADES is a small ice flow with a steep, 20 ft. wall at the base followed by a 60 ft. low angle slab, and a small bulge at the top.

FWA: Jose Abeyta, Dick Peterson and John Dedenski, December 14, 1980.

TRUMP CARD II 3

Around the corner to the left of the rock buttress where ACE OF SPADES is located there are two more short ice flows. After a 10 ft. steep face, follow a right ascending ramp to trees. Move up right through the trees, continuing on the second pitch of ACE OF SPADES if desired.

FA: Rick Wilcox and Roger Martin, Winter 1976.

OVERBID II 4+

The farthest right flow features an almost free-standing 60 ft. column of ice. Climb the column to mixed rock above.

FRA: Jose Abeyta and Dick Peterson, December 14, 1980.

ACE OF SPADES II 4

The climb is located a few hundred yards north of the giant landslide scar on the Mt. Lafayette side of Franconia Notch across from Profile Lake. Wander up through the woods for about a half mile and the ice will appear at the head of a long avalanche scar. Climb a strenuous vertical ice wall to a belay cave. Either climb an ice pillar on the left, or move right to easier ice bulges above.
FA: Rainsford and Tim Rouner, Winter 1974-75.

MT. GARFIELD

Mt. Garfield is the next major peak north of Mt. Lafayette and has several excellent climbs on its southwest face. The principle difficulty in winter climbing on Mt. Garfield is found in the approach, which involves a five mile hike, the difficulty of which depends entirely on trail conditions. The trailhead is reached by leaving Route 3 0.3 miles south of its intersection with Trudeau Rd. (often called "Five Corners," this is about seven miles north of Cannon Mt.). Avoiding a right fork, follow the Gale River Loop Rd. south for 1.2 miles, then swing left and cross a bridge to a parking lot on the right. Road conditions will vary depending again on snowfall.

THE BIG ONE III 5

The centerpiece flow on Mt. Garfield. Two pitches of hard ice climbing.
FA: Bradley White and Jim Shimberg, Winter 1987.

POSTHOLE ALFONSO II 4+

Left of THE BIG ONE, up the slab to a belay ledge, then up the headwall.
FA: Jim Shimberg and Bradley White, Winter 1986.

UNNAMED II 4

Climbs a flow at the far left end of the cliff.
FA: Jim Shimberg and Bradley White, Winter 1986.

MAD DOG II 5

Flow to the right of THE BIG ONE.
FA: Bradley White and Jim Shimberg, Winter 1987.

SICK PUP II 4+

Route description unknown.
FA: Jim Shimberg and Bradley White, Winter 1988.

BAKER RIVER VALLEY

Location: Rt. 25 west of Plymouth, NH to Rumney Village. Newfound lake is 20 minutes south off Rt. 3A.

Routes: All grades, typically short and steep, often thin.

Access: Park at base, 5-20 minute approach.

Descent: Rappel or easy walk off.

Weather: *"Valley"* sunny, see pg. 18.

Equipment: Standard ice rack, some rock gear.

Highlights: Great roadside cragging, *Scottish Gully, Selsun Blue, Learning Disabilities, Geographic Factor.*

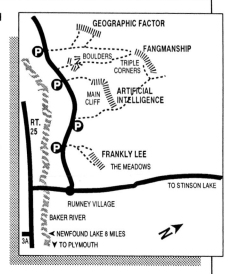

The Baker River Valley stretches northwest from Plymouth to Piermont, N.H. Modern ice climbing began here in the early 1970's but remained off the beaten path until recently, primarily due to the confusing approaches and a lack of published information on new routes. In the late 1980's and early 1990's the area gained a reputation for being one of New Hampshire's great rock cragging areas. This led to increased activity in the winter and now the area is well known for its great ice cragging as well.

NEWFOUND LAKE

Newfound Lake is located about eight miles southwest of Plymouth. From Route 93 take the exit for Route 25. Follow Route 25 for about three miles and then turn south on Route 3A and follow that road for approximately 5 miles to the East Hebron Road. Turn right and travel to Hebron Common. A general store will be on your right and Lake Shore Drive on your left. Head left on Lake

Shore Drive until the road meets the lake on the left. The ice will be obvious on the right.

The area is characterized by massive flows and very short approaches. Park wherever you can find room and approach the climbs up the scree. Descent for all routes is to the south (left) along the edge of the cliff and then down a wooded gully. Routes are listed left to right.

RED HEADWALL I 5
A headwall of steep pillars. Up the pillars to a slab leading to the top.
FA: Chris Hassig, Brian Brodeur, 1977.

BLOODLINE I 3
Named for some developments in knuckle technique. It is 30 feet right of the RED HEADWALL. Climb up the apron to a corner. Exit the corner on the right and continue up ramps to a belay in the trees.
FA: Ron Reynolds and Mark King, 1977.

PIKE LINE I 4
Right of BLOODLINE and 50 feet left of DUOFOLD a small steep ribbon of ice drops out of rock slabs above. Climb the ice and rock above to the trees.
FA: Chris Hassig and Bob Pike, 1977.

SLIM JIM I 3+-4 5.6
Right of PIKE LINE, start near the road and climb a verglas slab to a short pillar and overlap. Bring rock gear.
FA: Jim Shimberg, solo, January, 1990.

DUOFOLD I 4
One hundred feet from the right edge of the cliff, begin in a large corner with a headwall at its top. Climb ice leading left and up the headwall.
FA: Bob Pike and Chris Hassig, 1977.

RATTLESNAKE MOUNTAIN

Seven miles west of Plymouth, N.H., on Route 25, turn right at the junction with Stinson Lake Road. It is just a short drive from there to the center of Rumney village. From the town common, take the first left onto Buffalo Road. Travel a mile to reach the first climbing area, The Meadows. Park along the roadside and walk through a small meadow to the ice. Routes are listed right to left. Rattlesnake Mountain is a complex area with many short cliff bands scattered over the hillside. Even with the leaves off the trees it can be a hard place to navigate. Areas and routes will be described from right to left (approximately) beginning at THE MEADOW. Unless otherwise noted, routes are easy to rappel, or simply walk off to the sides of the cliff band.

THE MEADOW I 3-5

This area combines easy access with a high concentration of short routes on a large group of pillars and bulges. The original line climbs the cleft in the center. This is a great area for top-roping and the descent is a straightforward walk-off.
FA: John Rankin, Chris Hassig and Dave Foster, 1972.

GRADE 3 I 3

Located 80 feet left of THE MEADOW. A small snow gully leads to an ice headwall. Belay in trees. Descend to the right.
FA: Chris Hassig, John Rankin and Dave Foster, 1972.

SCOTTISH GULLY I 3

This is the obvious route to the right of CENTERFOLD. Highly Recommended.
FA: Unknown.

CENTERFOLD I 3

Located 200 feet left and uphill from THE MEADOW. A steep ramp in the middle of a short face. Climb to the trees (70'). Descend by rappel or downclimb left.
FA: Chris Hassig and Dave Foster, 1972.

GALAPAGOS I 5

About 75 feet left of CENTERFOLD locate the route FRANKY LEE on an obvious steep wall. GALAPAGOS and BARBADOS form infrequently just to the right. GALAPAGOS climbs very thin ice right of Barbados. Bring nuts and thin pitons.
FA: Jim Shimberg and Gary Heath, February, 1991.

BARBADOS I 5

Climbs the flow just right of Franky Lee. Often thin.
FA: Bradley White and partner, 1987.

FRANKY LEE I 5
Located 75 feet left of the CENTERFOLD. A steep wall of pillars and hummocks provide some unique and sustained climbing (90'). Belay in trees. It is usually in questionable condition. It is best to rappel
FA: Chris Hassig and Brian Brodeur, 1977.

PRIVATE EYE I 4+
Located left of the previous routes in the meadows. Take the left fork in the approach trail and head uphill for about 150 feet. Private Eye climbs a 40 foot sheet of ice. Rappel from a fixed anchor or walk off right. There is also a grade 2+/3 gully to the left of PRIVATE EYE which is recommended.
FA: Jim Shimberg, solo, January, 1991.

The next climbs are located on the ORANGE CRUSH CLIFF and the MAIN CLIFF and are approached from a parking lot on the north side of Buffalo Road 1.1 mile west of Stinson Road. The trail heads uphill toward the right side of the main cliff. There is a gully that separates the two cliffs providing an easy means of descent.

MANDIBLE I 3+
This climb is located on the right side of the Orange Crush Wall. Climb a verglassed slab to a short headwall of ice. Descend to the right.
FA:Jim Shimberg, solo, Winter ,1992.

JAWS PILLAR I 5
A rarely formed route to the left of MANDIBLE. Even when formed expect very hard and poorly protected climbing.
FA: Bradley White and Tom Bowker, late 1980's.

LEARNING DISABILITIES I 4
This route is located on the right end of the main cliff, up and to the left of the previous route. It is 75 feet left of a 200 foot overhanging wall. Climb through the two headwalls to the trees (150'). Descend the gully on the right side of the cliff. Highly recommended.
FA: Chris Hassig and Bob Pike, 1976.

VENEER I 4
Located 50 feet left of LEARNING DISABILITIES, it is never more than 1 inch thick when it does come into shape. Climb the thin slab to a bulge and belay on a ledge. Climb the ramp to the headwall and belay in the trees.

Descend as for LEARNING DISABILITIES.
FA: Brian Brodeur and Chris Hassig, 1977.

ARTIFICIAL INTELLIGENCE I 5 5.8
This route is located 80 feet left and downhill from VENEER, just before the ground begins to rise. It consists of a group of occasionally connected ice hummocks and runnels and provides an interesting mixed route. Climb up steep rock on mixed ground to the left end of a corner leading to a belay ledge on the edge of a prow. Climb the rock and ice above to the uppermost pillar on the headwall and the top. Descend as for LEARNING DISABILITIES.
FA: Chris Hassig, Mark Iber, 1978.

The next four routes are located west of the Main Cliff where a large flow drops out of an enclosed gully. Park a couple of hundred yards farther north on Buffalo Road, just past the left end of the Main Cliff; the ice should be visible through the trees. Follow the easiest path straight up through the woods.

THE CAVE ROUTE I 3
Climbs the ice inside the gully to the trees for 75 feet. Rappel.
FA: Chris Hassig and Bob Pike, 1976.

SELSUN BLUE I 4
Immediately left of THE CAVE ROUTE is a broad flow consisting of a series of steps. Descend left or rappel THE CAVE ROUTE.
FA: Bob Pike and Chris Hassig, 1976.

DANDRUFF I 4-
This rarely formed route climbs verglass between SELSUN BLUE and PSORIASIS. Rock gear needed. Descend as for the previous routes.
FRA: Jim Shimberg and Jim Hagan, February, 1989.

PSORIASIS I 5
A separate icicle left of SELSUN BLUE which has only formed once.
FA: Chris Hassig and Tim Gotwols, 1977.

To access the next group of climbs, walk up the road until just before it takes an obvious turn to the left. There will be a trail on the right that leads up through the Blackjack Boulders (you can't miss them). Continue straight ahead up through scree and trees aiming for a prominent hanging pillar; FANGMANSHIP. The first two routes are located several hundred feet right.

Rattlesnake Mountain's many routes and easy access make it a popular cragging destination. Here, Tom Coe starts up SELSUN BLUE.

Photo by Jim Shimberg

HULA HOOP I 4+ 5.7

Above the Blackjack Boulders, head east (right) past the FANGMANSHIP wall to the left end of a cliff called the Waimea Wall. At times there are three ice flows in this area. Hula Hoop climbs the left-hand flow and offers sustained mixed climbing. Bring thin pitons, rock gear and short screws. Descend right.
FA: Jim Shimberg and Mike Johnson, February, 1991.

POLAR PILE I 4

This route is located in the Triple Corners area above the Blackjack Boulders and between HULA HOOP and FANGMANSHIP. It climbs short, steep headwalls.
FA: Jim Shimberg and Jeff Eckert, Winter 1991.

K-9 I 4

Two hundred feet right and uphill of FANGMANSHIP there is a corner with an ice ribbon dropping down. Climb the ice ribbon (typically mixed ground) to trees and the top. The easiest descent is by rappel.
FA: Chris Hassig and Bob Pike, 1977.

ICE-OLATOR I 4

This climb is located between K-9 and FANGMANSHIP. Go up a snow ramp to a short headwall. Typically thin. Descend the woods on either side.
FA: Ted Hammond and Dave Karl, 1982.

FANGMANSHIP I 5

A route rarely in suitable shape. Climb the wide left-leaning ramp to a large platform at the base of the pillar. Climb the pillar slab above to trees (180 foot pitch). Walk off up and left to the northwest and down a gully. The headwall to the right of the normal route has also been climbed.
FA: Chris Hassig and Bob Pike, 1978.

For the next collection of climbs, continue west on Buffalo Road for a couple of hundred feet to a pull-out on the left just before the road begins to go uphill. It is possible to view the routes from an opening in the woods across the street from the house. Follow a faint trail up through the woods for about fifteen minutes to reach this cliff.

The first routes to be described here are located to the right of the gully. To descend from these routes, either head down and to the right (difficult) or rappel with two ropes off large trees above THE GEOGRAPHIC FACTOR.

PRESTOR PILLAR I 5
   This is the farthest route to the right. Climb the continuous pillar to a ledge just below the trees.
FA: Tim Gotwols and Chris Hassig, 1977.

JOHN'S PILLAR I 5-
   Climb the seldom-formed pillar between Prestor John and Prestor Pillar.
FA: Jim Shimberg and Joel O'Connell, Winter, 1992.

PRESTOR JOHN I 4
   Immediately right of THE GEOGRAPHIC FACTOR, ascend a steep series of steps to a belay in the trees.
FA: Tim Gotwols and Chris Hassig, 1977.

THE GEOGRAPHIC FACTOR I 5
   A series of steep, stacked pillars flowing out of an overhanging basaltic dike create some unique airy climbing conditions. One of the most spectacular routes in the region.
FA: Tim Gotwols, Brian Brodeur, and Chris Hassig, 1977.

   The next three routes are found about a hundred yards farther west from THE GEOGRAPHIC FACTOR. Traverse left passing three gullies to a final snow gully capped by an overhang and with an ice wall on its left.

DUSTBOWL I 3+ 5.6
   Climb frozen turf to a short, steep headwall and then up to the top.
FRA: Jim Shimberg and Pete Gamache, Winter 1989.

SASQUATCH I 5-
   Start on the lower left side of the flow and diagonal up to and over the headwall; continue on slabs to the trees.
FA: Bob Pike and Ron Reynolds, 1978.

SOFFIT BREATH I 4
   Up the gully 50 feet to a ribbon of ice which flows down the corner of the gully. Climb ice to the trees just below the gully's top.
FA: Chris Hassig, 1982.

OLIVARIAN NOTCH

Owl's Head Cliff is located in Olivarian Notch, 18 miles west of Plymouth on Route 25. From the boat landing parking area, approach the cliff through a frozen swamp on the left side of the wall.

Note: The cliff is in the National Forest; however, the land at its base is a nesting ground for birds of prey and climbing activity of any kind should be avoided in warm weather.

SNAKE ATTACK III 4
Climb the large flow in the center of the cliff up and right to the trees. An 800 foot climb. The left end of the wall ices up forming a large slab and has not been climbed as yet.
FA: Chris Hassig, 1979.

THE FEAR OF LIVING DANGEROUSLY II 4+
The left side of the cliff is characterized by two big flows. This route climbs the right-hand flow for four pitches. Very thin and delicate climbing is found throughout, with the crux being free-standing icicles through overlaps on the second pitch. Bring rock pro.
FA: Dougald McDonald and Carlton Schneider, January, 1986.

KINSMAN NOTCH

Kinsman Notch is located on Route 112 about five miles west of North Woodstock, N.H. Just a mile or so past the junction with Route 118, a number of interesting climbs will be found on the south side of the road on the northeast side of Mt. Waternomee. The approach takes about twenty minutes.

Kinsman Notch was a favorite haunt for a number of climbers living in the Plymouth area in the mid 1970's, some of them students at Plymouth State College. Most of the routes in this area were climbed at that time by: Bob Pike, Ron Reynolds, Chris Hassig, Ted Hammond, Dave Karl, Mark Iber, George Lutz and others. Althought lacking clear documentation, it is likely that most of the routes in this area were first ascended by members of this group.

LUCK O' THE IRISH I 4+

On Route 112, approximately a mile west of the junction with Route 118, is a 150 foot green gully on the north side of the road. This is a big wide flow with a number of independent lines possible. All are about the same difficulty.
FA: Unknown.

BLARNEY STONE I 3

Approximately 80 yards east of LUCK O' THE IRISH is a two pitch iced-up slab. The final bulge is the crux.
FRA: Dick Peterson and Jose Albeyta, January, 1981.

LEPRECHAUN'S LAMENT I 2-3+

Approximately 400 yards west of LUCK O' THE IRISH is a wide flow about 90 feet high. Three separate lines are possible on this flow: the ramps on the left and right (both grade 2), and a direct line up the center which has steep walls at the top and bottom connected by a ramp.
FA: Unknown.

KILARNEY I 2

Forty yards west of LEPRECHAUN'S LAMENT is a one pitch flow consisting of low-angle ice bulges.
FA: Unknown.

POT 'O GOLD I 4

Fifty yards right of KILARNEY is a short climb which begins with a 30 foot vertical pillar.
FA: Unknown.

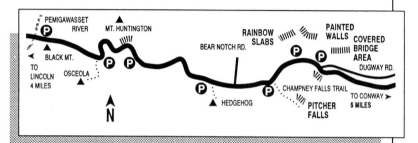

Location:	Rt. 112, 30 miles from Lincoln to Conway, NH.	**Equipment:**	Standard ice rack, some rock gear.
Routes:	All grades, lots of easy ice.	**Highlights:**	*Rainbow Slabs*, great practice area; *Pitcher Falls* secluded, beautiful; *Way in the Wilderness*, classic hard route.
Access:	Pull-outs along road, 5 minutes to 1 hour approach.		
Descent:	Rappel or walk off, some bushwhacking.	**Warning:**	No fuel or food facilities between Lincoln and Conway.
Weather:	*"Valley"*, see page 18.		

Stretching from Lincoln to Conway N.H., the scenic Kancamagus Highway contains a variety of secluded, yet highly entertaining ice climbing areas. Ranging from the moderate RAINBOW SLABS, to the extreme WAY IN THE WILDERNESS, to the quiet beauty of PITCHER FALLS, "The Kanc" has something for everyone. Since they don't get the volume of traffic that the more popular areas do, climbs along the Kancamagus typically involve some bushwhacking on skis or snowshoes on the approaches. But the solitude and beauty found here makes all the effort worthwhile. Please note; there are no gas stations or stores between Lincoln and Conway (30 miles). Areas will be described from west to east.

BLACK MOUNTAIN

LONG WAY HOME III 2-3

The center of the three gentle, broad ice flows opposite the Wilderness

Trail trailhead. After two to three mile approach, climb six to eight pitches of enjoyable, low-angled ice.
FA: Brad White and Doug C. Burnell, February, 1978.

MOUNT OSCEOLA

ON THE DROOL OF THE BEAST II 5-

This hard, one pitch route is located in Mad River Notch and approached via the Greely Ponds Trail which leaves the south side of the Kancamagus Highway a couple of miles west of the height-of-land at Kancamagus Pass, and near an obvious hairpin turn. Hike or ski in about a mile and a half until just past the high point, then angle toward Osceola. Climb the steep, skinny ice flow which at first is in a squeeze chimney.
FA: Kurt Winkler and George Hurley, January, 1982.

MOUNT HUNTINGTON

SHEER ELEGANCE II 4+ 5.6

This climb is located on the very obvious wall facing the Kancamagus on the southeast face of the lower summit of Mt. Huntington. Park at the "Pemi Overlook" parking area just west of the height-of-land at Kancamagus Pass and walk straight in to the cliff. Begin in the middle of the cliff in a right facing corner. The first pitch is mixed, up a column to an overhang, escape right on rock, then back left to ice, then up the gully to belay on left. Then follow the gully up and right to thin ice and the top. On the first ascent protection was so bad on the second pitch that there was groundfall potential from 200 feet up!
FA: Brad White, Todd Swain and Jack Wenzel, January, 1985.

MOUNT HEDGEHOG

CHOCKSTONE CHIMLEY II 3 5.6

Named for a speech impediment, this is a one hundred foot mixed route in Helms Deep Gully on the south face of Mt. Hedgehog. Thirteen miles west of Conway, follow the U.N.H. Trail for 2 1/2 miles to the crag. Combined with

other routes on the same cliff, this is potentially a worthwhile undertaking. In a gully to the east of the summit ledges, climb a steep slab to a chockstone in a chimney, by-pass it on the left to a ledge with a small tree, and rock climb up a corner (5.6) to the finish.
FA: Todd Swain, January 8, 1981.

PITCHER FALLS

PITCHER FALLS II 3-4+

A beautiful and secluded practice area in an unusual chasm. Eleven miles west of Conway park at the trailhead of the Champney Falls Trail. The approach takes about forty minutes if the trail has been packed. The falls offer a number of possible routes of varying degrees of difficulty. Trees provide secure anchors. An interesting two pitch girdle traverse is also possible at about grade 4.
FA: George Hurley, Bradley and Philip Platt climbed the main flow on December 30, 1979. Hurley returned on February 3, 1980, and climbed an upper section (Grade 1) with Chap Fischera, Jim Saybo, and Bill Zelop. Peter Yost and Jim Graham did the girdle traverse on February 24, 1983, and John Tremblay and Joe Lentini visited the area in the mid 1980's and led some extremely steep and thin climbs. All routes here can easily be top-roped.

CRACK IN THE WOODS CLIFF

This hidden cliff is a favorite getaway for rock climbers and has a couple of worthwhile ice routes as well. It is located in the woods just west of Rainbow Slabs. Park at a pull-out 1.3 miles west of the Covered Bridge. Cross the Swift River, turn right on the Nanamocomuck Ski Trail for a short distance, and then turn left and head up into the woods for about fifteen minutes to reach the crag.

COLUMN IN THE WOODS I 4

Left of the obvious corner is a steep icefall. Rappel the route.
FA: Kurt Winkler and Chris Hassig, March 4, 1982.

BOSSANOVA I 3

The next ice flow to the left. Rappel the route or descend left.
FA: Chris Hassig, solo, March 4, 1982.

ANGELS DON'T SHATTER I 3
Left of BOSSANOVA is a thin ice wave. Descend left.
FA: Kurt Winkler, solo, March 4, 1982.

RAINBOW SLABS

RAINBOW SLABS I 2-3 (3+ 5.4 A0 — girdle traverse)
This sunny practice area offers many possibilities for beginning and intermediate ice climbers. The slabs are easily seen from the road as a wide,
rectangular cliff band and are usually covered with blue ice. Many flows will be
found here giving one to three pitches of forty to sixty degree water ice. To
descend, rappel off trees with two ropes. Just west of the parking lot for Lower
Falls the Rainbow Slabs are visible across the river from a convenient
roadside turn-off. Cross the Swift River turn right for a short distance along the
Nanamocomuck Ski Trail, then angle left on overgrown logging roads to the
base of the cliff. In addition to the main face, there are a few more short,
moderate ice flows on the slabs between Rainbow Slabs and The Painted
Walls. A right to left girdle traverse has been completed to the central flow.
*FA: Unknown. Kurt Winkler, Shraddha Howard and Drubha Hein climbed the
girdle traverse in February 1992.*

THE PAINTED WALLS

High above and to the right of RAINBOW SLABS is a striking cliff lined
with vertical stripes, THE PAINTED WALLS. On the left side of the cliff is a
distinct dihedral that in a good season will be choked full of ice. The approach
is a long uphill bushwack, but fortunately the condition of the route can usually
be determined from the road.

WAY IN THE WILDERNESS III 5
One of the most beautiful climbs in the White Mountains. Park at the Lower
Falls parking lot. Cross the Swift River and head up a very steep hill to an
amphitheater at the climb's base. Because of its south-facing location, the
route needs optimum conditions to form and there is a constant danger from
falling ice. Ascend a series of vertical sections on occasionally candled ice to
a comfortable rock belay on the left with fixed anchors.
Step out onto a steep pillar, climb into a V-groove, and finish up the final

Paul Boissonneault climbing one of the region's most beautiful lines, WAY IN THE WILDERNESS, up a series of mushroomed pillars in a huge corner system.

Photo by Steve Larson

lower-angled gully. Rappel the route with two ropes, or walk around the cliff to the left end.

FA: Jim Dunn, Michael Hartrich and Peter Cole, February, 1978.

THE COVERED BRIDGE AREA

THE COVERED BRIDGE ICE FLOWS I 3-5

A convenient practice area right next to the road as well as some harder options on neighboring crags make this area attractive. Park at the bridge, walk through it and you'll soon see a few ice flows on your left as you walk down Dugway Rd. These offer good bouldering and top rope problems. Sundown Ledge, behind the Covered Bridge campground is also worth exploring.

FA: Unknown.

WINTERLUDE II 3 +

From the Covered Bridge, walk back towards Conway on Route 112 (the Kancamagus Highway) for 1/4 mile or so and you will see a flash of blue in the trees to the south. Cross a small stream and walk uphill 200 yds. to a small crag. WINTERLUDE is the most prominent flow on the crag, ascending the 100 ft. high cliff near the left hand end.

FA: Kurt Winkler and Joe Perez, February 22, 1979.

ICE CAPADES I 3

Approximately 75 feet left of WINTERLUDE, go up an ice ramp to a tree, then climb up and left in a mixed groove to a ledge and continue to woods.

FA: Todd Swain and Jim Frangos, January 17, 1983.

QUALUDE (IT'S WORTH THE TRIP) I 5

About 300 feet right of WINTERLUDE look for an easy icy groove heading up and left which is climbed to a ledge. The second pitch climbs verglass to the woods. Descend by rappel.

FA: Todd Swain and Jim Frangos, January 17, 1983.

ICE FALLIES I 4

Further to the right is another poorly protected route that begins up a short corner and finishes up a short, steep icicle to a slab.

FA: Todd Swain and Jim Frangos, January 17, 1983.

SACO RIVER VALLEY

Location: Main area, Cathedral Ledge, 2 miles off Rt. 302, North Cownay, NH.

Routes: All grades, many hard classics, great beginner areas.

Access: Park near base, 10 minutes to 1/2 hour approach.

Descent: Rappel or easy walk off, auto road down Cathedral.

Weather: *"Valley"* sunny, see pg. 18.

Equipment: Rock gear very useful for longer routes.

Highlights: Classic routes; *Repentence, Remission, Myth of Sisyphus, Black Pudding Gully.* Many other areas from N. Conway to Crawford Notch.

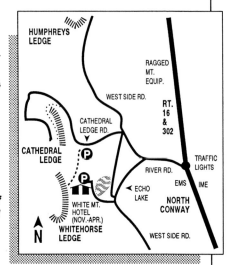

The Saco River Valley is one of the most scenic areas in New Hampshire. In the twenty-five miles from its head at the top of Crawford Notch, the Saco River changes character from a rushing brook spilling over boulders in the narrow notch, to a wide, gentle stream that meanders through the farmland underneath the cliffs of North Conway. Several years ago, to boost tourism in the area, the local chamber of commerce adapted the designation of *Mt Washington Valley* for this area and unfortunately it stuck. For this guidebook, however, we will return to the more appropriate designation of Saco River Valley.

Some of the best known, and hardest ice climbing in New England is found in the lower stretches of this valley on Cathedral, Whitehorse, and Humphrey's Ledges. Streaked each winter with ice, these dramatic granite cliffs are an unforgettable sight. Short approaches, the relative lack of objective danger, and generally more hospitable weather only add to the attraction of this popular ice climbing area.

Running north from these major cliffs, Route 302 parallels the Saco River, and good ice climbing is to be found all along this beautiful valley. Areas in this section will be described from south to north, before coming to the next section at Frankenstein Cliff in Crawford Notch State Park.

The town of North Conway, with its many amenities, is a convenient center only a few miles from Cathedral and Whitehorse. Lodging, food and drink, bargains at the factory outlet stores on the infamous "strip" and the latest information on climbing conditions are all readily available. Stop by any of the three local climbing shops for information.

To reach the ledges from North Conway, turn west on the River Road and drive about a mile to the cliffs. There is plenty of parking at the far end of the chalet development below Cathedral Ledge. Routes in the Saco River Valley will be described from south to north, beginning with three easy climbs on the flanks of Middle and South Moat Mountains, just south of Whitehorse Ledge.

Winter ascents of summer rock routes in this section are noted for historical value only. First winter ascents of rock routes are described with the initials *FWA*. Accurate route descriptions can be found in the rock climbing guides to the area.

MOAT RANGE

RED EAGLE BROOK ICE FALL II 1
This brook starts high on the east side of South Moat Mountain and provides a longer and easier climb than does Willey's Slide in Crawford Notch. It is a place for a beginner to practice French technique in absolute privacy. Trees beside the brook provide all needed belays. Even a few inches of snow will obscure the ice. From the north edge of the gravel pit on High Street (off the Passaconaway Road, also called the Dugway Road), follow a logging road west to Red Eagle Brook (1 mile); the road ends at the brook. Follow the brook upstream to the ice fall. The approach takes about 30 minutes from the gravel pit.
FA: George Hurley and John Bickford, February 9, 1980.

MOAT MOUNTAIN ICE FALL II 2
This climb is about 300 feet of easy to moderate ice. The ice fall is on the

east side of Middle Moat Mountain and can be seen from the center of North Conway.

To reach the climb, drive south on West Side Road to the Passaconaway (or Dugway) Road; then west until near the Conway/Albany town line; turn north on High Street to the end of the road. "End of the road" may be at the end of the plowed and inhabited part of High Street, or at a Forest Service barrier (.2 mi. farther) just east of a gravel pit, or .8 mi. farther at the actual road end. From a clear-cut logged area where the road ends, bushwack northwest to a stream bed. Follow this west to the ice fall. With good conditions the walk takes about 30 minutes from the clearcut to the ice fall. If you must walk the maximum distance the approach would take about an hour. If there is deep snow, don't bother with this route .

FA: George Hurley and Chris McElheny, December 17, 1979.

HANCOCK FALLS I 1

This ice fall is in a hidden basin midway between the summits of Birch Hill and Middle Moat Mt. on the stream which starts just east of the top of Middle Moat Mt. The easiest approach is by skis from Ledge View Dr. in the N.W. end of the Birch Hill housing development off West Side Road a mile south of Whitehorse Ledge. Snowmobiles usually pack out the trail to within about one hundred yards of the falls.

FA: George and Jean Hurley, January 22, 1982.

WHITEHORSE LEDGE

The varying terrain characteristic of Whitehorse Ledge offers the climber two types of winter climbing. The east facing slabs occasionally ice up enough in the middle and upper sections to give a long and fairly committing mixed route. Poor protection and wind slab avalanche conditions add to these routes a degree of seriousness which other areas such as WILLEY'S SLIDE usually lack. Slab avalanches of three to four feet thick are not at all uncommon during heavy snow years.

The South Buttress of Whitehorse presents an entirely different profile; here steep rock faces up to 500 feet high infrequently ice up to form ice routes of 3-4 pitches in length. These routes are only possible after prolonged spells of sub-zero weather. Climbs are described right to left beginning with the slabs.

Park at the southwest corner of the chalet development beneath Cathedral and walk south on a wide, usually packed out, trail towards the cliff. After passing John Bouchard's Climbers' Cabin, follow a hiking trail (not always tracked) to the avalanche debris at the foot of the slabs. Climbs on the South Buttress are 10-20 minutes farther left. To descend from the top of the slabs, or from any routes that top out on the South Buttress, follow the Bryce Path north and descend from the top of Whitehorse to the saddle next to Cathedral, then stay on the marked trail back down to the cabin.

BEGINNER'S ROUTE II 2-3

A poorly protected, snow-covered rock climb, that climbs straight up about a hundred feet left of the right-hand margin of the slabs. Summer belays are all from bolts, but don't count on finding them.
FWA: Unknown.

STANDARD ROUTE III 3-4

A classic mixed route and probably the best climb on the slabs in winter. Follow the thinly ice and snow-covered slabs up to the arch, and climb this to Lunch Ledge. Then climb any of the several ice flows through the final overlaps depending on which one is in condition. Some aid may be necessary here.
FWA: David Bernays and Andrew Griscom, February 7, 1954.

THE SLABS DIRECT III 4

A poorly protected mixed route in the center of the slabs. Climbs two pitches up Whitehorse SLABS DIRECT (the summer route between STANDARD and BEGINNER'S) to the Standard Route Arch. Climb over the arch on steep verglassed slabs and connect with a prominent blue ice flow on the final dike of SLIDING BOARD. Climb a short vertical pillar to the upper slabs. Both the start and the upper pillar had been climbed before.
FA: Ed Webster and Butch Constantine made the direct route over the arch in March, 1982.

SLIDING BOARD III 4 5.7

Another difficult and poorly protected mixed route. Climb to the base of the arch and then follow the summer route, paralleling the arch for two pitches to an obvious left facing corner, then straight up to the final headwall.
FWA: Jeff Pheasant, 1978.

WEDGE III 4 5.6

In the same category as SLIDING BOARD. Wait for thick conditions.

Ascends the smooth face left of SLIDING BOARD eventually traversing left on a tree ledge to the final upper slabs.
FWA: Unknown.

AN ALCHEMIST'S DREAM III 4
On the right of The Ceiling, a large horizontal roof seen just left of where the slabs and the South Buttress meet, is a long, multi-pitch ice climb with a tenuous, free-standing ice column at the start. Ascend low-angled ice to the ceiling, belay, then move out right onto the column, the crux. Work up easier slabs to trees and follow the ice flow to the top of the cliff, over a steep step on the fourth pitch.
FA: Clint Cummins and John Imbrie climbed the column in January, 1978, before the leader took a very serious fall. Ken Andrasko and George Reiser completed the route the following weekend.

ENDANGERED SPECIES III 4+ 5.7-8
Due to poor protection, this is a serious mixed route. Climb the isolated ice flow right in the center of the South Buttress, just to the left of the CHILDREN'S CRUSADE dike, about fifty feet left of the obvious 5.4 dihedral start to BEELZEBUB. Pitons and Friends may be helpful. Face climb up the ERADI-CATE dike for two pitches, making the transition to ice on the second lead. On the third pitch, ice climb out right past moderate bulges, then climb verglas and rivulets of ice diagonally right to the traverse ledge of the GIRDLE TRAV-ERSE. At this point, the first ascent party traversed right and rappelled off.
FA: Ed Webster and Kurt Winkler made the first ascent in January, 1982. EB's were worn on the first pitch and the crux ice lead was done in the dark.

THE ELIMINATE IV 5.8, A3
A long and demanding artificial climb. Richey was just sixteen years old when he accomplished this important ascent.
FWA: Mark Richey, solo, January, 1975.

SOUTH BUTTRESS DIRECT IV 5.8, A3 (to date, 5.11, AO)
A long and difficult mixed route in winter. Rarely repeated.
FWA: Jeff Pheasant made the first ascent of the climb, solo, over a period of several weeks in the winter of 1976.

THE MYTH OF SISYPHUS IV 5
Rarely in shape due to a southern exposure, THE MYTH is the prominent vertical ice ribbon to the right of the INFERNO route on the left side of the South

Buttress. It is climbable only after sustained periods of very cold weather. Scramble up an easy ice groove, then hike left to reach the base. Three pitches of delicate, sustained, poorly protected ice climbing lead to the top of the flow. After the second pitch, it is possible to escape right up mixed ground. Carry several pitons and nuts.

FA: Rainsford and Tim Rouner made the first ascent of the first two leads and traversed off right in February of 1976. The direct finish, the crux, was completed by Kurt Winkler and Ed Webster in January, 1982.

THE GIRDLE TRAVERSE OF WHITEHORSE LEDGE IV 3-4 5.9 A0
A very long mixed climb across the entire cliff. Over 2000' of alpine conditions from the slabs around to the South Buttress.
FWA: Doug Madara and Bill Kane, February, 1977.

GUIDE'S WALL

Between Whitehorse and Cathedral is a small cliff called the Guide's Wall. The following climbs are hidden in the woods between the two cliffs. Approach as for Whitehorse and bushwhack up right from the lower right edge of the Whitehorse slabs.

ON THIN ICE I 2-3
This is the first climb you will come to up and right of BEGINNER'S ROUTE on Whitehorse and left of SEASON'S GREETINGS. Up low-angled slabs and thin ice to below a steep bulge. Traverse right to a hemlock tree.
FA: Todd Swain and Ed Keller, January 3, 1983.

SEASON'S GREETINGS I 3
An obscure but well worthwhile route that begins on a low-angled slab, climbs to a bulge at ten feet and then finishes up a 70 degree slab for a full pitch.
FA: Tiger Burns and Butch Constantine, December 18, 1982.

SOLDIER OF FORTUNE I 3
Below the Guide's Wall and slightly left, but still to the right of SEASON'S GREETINGS. Climb the obvious thin flow from the bottom to the top with marginal protection. The first ascent party literally came under live fire when someone below the cliff began shooting off tree branches with a high powered rifle!
FA: Todd Swain and Ed Keller, January 3, 1983.

THE MYTH OF SISYPHUS, a fitting name for this elusive route. Often sighted but rarely climbed, "The Myth" is one of the most ephemeral routes in the area. Seen as a glinting line on cold mornings, it is usually gone by lunch. Here Doug Madara works his way up the poorly protected and thin first pitch while attempting the second ascent in 1982.
Photo by S. Peter Lewis

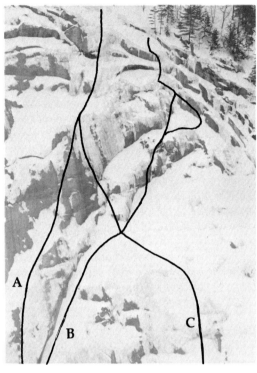

Whitehorse Ledge The Slabs Area

A.	SLIDING BOARD	4 5.7	101
B.	STANDARD ROUTE	3-4	101
C.	SLABS DIRECT	4	101

D.	AN ALCHEMIST'S DREAM	4	102
	(50 yards left of slabs left-hand margin)		

CATHEDRAL LEDGE

Cathedral Ledge offers easy access to some of the most challenging ice climbs in the Saco River Valley, and in fact in New England. In a good year, the cliff will be streaked from one end to the other with water ice, such as the year in which THIN AIR was done as an ice climb, but these years are rare. Each year, most of the cliff's finest ice routes are formed by mid-January. The summer tourist road is still the best approach in winter, except that it is not plowed beyond the second turn-off into the chalet development.Therefore, climbers normally park in the southwest corner of the development where there is ample room for many cars.The unplowed summit road offers quick access to all climbs on the cliff. Descend north along the trail skirting the cliff's edge to the North End or hike down the auto road. The climbs on Cathedral will be described from left to right, beginning with the upper left wall. For routes on this part of the cliff, the best approach is to ascend the auto road to the summit, then follow a climber's path south, skirting the cliff edge to a snow gully that leads to the very left-hand edge of the upper left wall. Traverse the ledge to reach your intended climb.

NUTCRACKER I 5
Under good conditions, a strenuous vertical sheet of ice will form over the summer route at the far upper left corner of the cliff.
FWA: Peter Cole, Bryan Becker and Mark Whiton, January, 1977.

DOUBLE VEE I 5
Similar to the other ice flows which infrequently form on Cathedral's upper left wall, a steep sheet one hundred feet right of NUTCRACKER.
FWA: Mark Whiton, 1977.

CHICKEN DELIGHT I 5
Another vertical pillar fifty feet right of DOUBLE VEE.
FWA: Kurt Winkler and George Hurley, 1982.

NOMAD CRACK II 5+
Beginning just right of CHICKEN DELIGHT, seventy-five feet of unrelenting vertical ice call for the proper mental attitude. Finish here or step out right and climbs another short vertical flow up to the woods.
FA: Kurt Winkler and Jim Tierney, February, 1982.

REFUSE II 3 5.5

The bottom of the ramp on upper REFUSE occasionally ices up. A worthwhile and moderate mixed route with good protection.
FA: Unknown.

Climbs will now be described left to right beginning at the lower left side of the cliff.

THREE BIRCHES II 4 5.8

Approach from directly below following faint paths to the lowest point of rock. A twenty foot right trending arch marks the start of the route. Exciting climbing up verglassed slabs just right of the arch, followed by mixed climbing leads to a clump of trees. Rappel, or follow a long, cold layback flake to the tree covered ledge.
FWA: Bill Kane and Mack Johnson, January, 1978.

FUNHOUSE I 5.7
POOH I 5.7

Both climbs provide good exercise in snow-covered rock climbing. Fifty feet right of THREE BIRCHES, FUNHOUSE begins in the right-hand of two parallel right facing corners, face climbs to a good ledge and then finishes up a steep face just left of POOH. POOH climbs just right of FUNHOUSE into a chimney with a hanging block, up to the ledge, and then moves left to finish up an obvious steep crack and face directly above the first pitch of FUNHOUSE.
FWA: Kim Smith, et al, January, 1978.

RECOMPENSE III 5.9

Another worthwhile winter ascent, primarily rock. Begins at the lowest point of rock below the tourist lookout just left of The Prow buttress. Follow cracks up and left to an obvious chimney and finish up the striking right facing corner just left of the top of THE PROW.
FWA: Henry Barber and friend, 1974.

THE PROW III 5.6 A2 (now 5.11+)

A recommended winter aid climb. Much of the route is fixed with pitons; please do not place any additional pins. A large selection of wired stoppers and some small Friends will be all you'll need. Follow a direct line up the very prow of the buttress using disconnected crack systems aiming for a triangular roof near the top of the cliff.
FWA: John Bouchard and Ajax Greene, December, 1974.

THE BIG FLUSH II 4

The large tree-filled corner which divides Cathedral Ledge in half provides an excellent mixed climb in winter. The route consists of ice flows separated by rock steps and trees and is harder than you would think.
FWA: Chris Noonan and Jeff Butterfield, Winter 1978.

GOOFER'S DIRECT II 3

Although the first forty feet can be thin and awkward to protect, GOOFER'S is one of the most popular routes of its grade. In one long pitch, or two short ones, climb the obvious sustained ice fall to the left of THIN AIR, near the base of THE BIG FLUSH. The route ends in a prominent bat-like cave. Rappel with two ropes from the cave, or traverse left and head down to the trees with one rope.
FA: John Bragg, John Bouchard and Henry Barber, Winter 1972-73.

SUPER GOOFER II 5-

The difficult direct finish. Climb one pitch of GOOFER'S and belay on the left at a tree. Continue up easy ground to the base of a prominent steep ice column with a protection piton at its base. Ascend the strenuous forty foot pillar to a belay ledge on the left. The crux involves delicate, thin ice above. When the ice ends, climb over moss and leaves to a tree belay. Finish up a steep groove to the fence at the top of the cliff.
FA: George Hurley and Les Gould, January 31, 1982.

THIN AIR III 5 5.6

On occasion, THIN AIR ices up providing a mixed route of a superb nature. In February of 1976, the ice covered the entire face; not a single rock move was made! These conditions have never returned since. Most climbers settle for a thin ice smear at the start, rock climbing to the two bolt belay above the traverse, and continue up the moderate ice flow at the top. Two hundred feet right of THE BIG FLUSH climb straight up for fifty feet to an obvious traverse line leading right. At its end climb straight up the face to the right facing corner and a good ledge. The last pitch goes straight up to the top of the cliff. Descend by walking off to the right and then up left through the woods to reach the road.
FWA: Michael Hartrich and Mark Whiton, February, 1976.

STANDARD ROUTE III 4 5.6

A true alpine classic whose severity in winter depends entirely upon the conditions. Should the cave wall be verglassed, the ascent can be very

difficult. Climbs the obvious chimney system that splits the center of the cliff right of Thin Air. After a narrow tear of ice at the start, mixed climbing leads to the cave. Climbing the notorious "cave wall" is the crux. Above, work up mixed snow and ice in the upper chimney to the top.
FWA: Hugo Stadtmuller and Henry W. Kendall, January 19, 1964.

DIAGONAL III 5 5.6
The crux of the summer rock climb, the final bulge, overflows with ice each winter to create a fifty foot vertical pillar. Climb up Standard until a dike on the right is reached that runs diagonally up and right across the blank wall. Rock climb for two pitches up the poorly protected dike at the start, then go for all the marbles up the column. A bit on the serious side. Two ropes are needed to retreat from this section of the cliff.
FWA: Chris Rowins and Tiger Burns, Winter 1977-78.

GRAND FINALE IV 5.8 A3
A winter wall climb with little ice. Begin about fifty feet downhill from STANDRAD. Dowels mark the start of this route which climbs mostly on aid for two pitches before crossing DIAGONAL and finishing over a steep bulge left of that route's chimney.
FWA: Alain Comeau, climbing solo, came very close to climbing the first winter ascent of the route before Steve Larson and Paul Boissonneault completed it in the winter of 1978-79.

MORDOR WALL IV 5 A4
An arduous combination of difficult aid and steep ice. Start right of GRAND FINALE at an obvious flake and shallow right facing corner. Aid (nuts only please) the corner to a hanging stance. Hook right across the blank wall to hard aid up a bashie ladder leading over the crest of the wall. From here aid up until the ice is reached and climb the massive ice flow to the top. There is a sustained vertical curtain near the top.
FWA: Bryan Becker and Alain Comeau over three days in January, 1979.

MORDOR/DIAGONAL LINK IV 5 A4
An intriguing link that breaks up and left from the end of the second pitch of the Mordor Wall to reach the lowest drip coming out of the DIAGONAL'S crux chimney. The connecting pitch was just a couple of inches thick on the first ascent and involved a completely unprotected run-out for 80 feet directly above the hanging belay. Finish up the column on DIAGONAL.
FRA: Pat Hackett and John Tremblay, winter 1986/87.

MINES OF MORIA IV 5.7 A2
Another hard wall route up the center of the cliff. Mostly rock.
FWA:Bryan Becker, Alain Comeau and Eric Engberg, January, 1977.

PENDULUM ROUTE IV 5.8 A2 (now 5.11)
A long and intricate winter climb, with an ice curtain hanging down off the roof.
FWA: Chris Hassig and Mark Whiton, Winter 1977.

FOREST OF FANGORN IV 5.7,A3
A long mixed route.
FWA: Steve Larson and Paul Boissonneault, Winter, 1979-80.

CATHEDRAL DIRECT III 3-4 5.7 A2
This is the next full length chimney system two hundred feet right of STANDARD ROUTE. Begin beneath the huge cave-like "cathedral," aid left along a horizontal crack to the back of the cathedral. The second pitch takes the wild thirty foot roof directly with much fixed gear. Above, follow the ice choked upper chimney for at least four more pitches to the top of the cliff.
FWA: Alain Comeau and Tony Trocchi, Winter 1976-77.

REPENTENCE III 5
The classic hard ice climb in the East with steep and sustained difficulties. The line ascends the left hand of two prominent ice-filled chimneys on the northern end of Cathedral Ledge, and is commonly done in either three or four pitches. The crux on the second lead can take a considerable amount of time to form and even then can be exceedingly hard if the column is candled or detached. Finish over an awkward chockstone just below the top. The first ascent of this route was a major breakthrough in difficulty for New England ice climbers.
FWA: John Bragg and Rick Wilcox, Winter 1973.

ANGEL'S HIGHWAY III 5.8 A2
The aid route that climbs the blank wall between REPENTENCE and REMISSION.
FWA: Peter Cole and Jeff Pheasant, Winter 1974-75.

REMISSION IV 5+ 5.7
The most difficult route on Cathedral Ledge, it ascends the right hand chimney (forty feet) right of REPENTENCE. An awkward mixed pitch (5.7) up

Bryan Becker on the sustained crux pillar of REMISSION. Etriers were used here for aid on the first ascent in 1976.

Photo by Ed Webster

a left-facing corner gains the base of the ice flow and a large belay ledge on the right. Continue up thin ice to another good stance on the right below the crux column. Swing onto the vertical pillar which is followed into the upper chimney and a ledge on the left. A short pitch leads to the woods.

FWA: Rainsford Rouner, Peter Cole and Timothy Rouner made the first winter ascent in January, 1976, using etriers on the crux column. Subsequent ascent parties have dispensed with these.

WARLOCK II 5.8 A4
Hard aid climbing to the right of REMISSION.
FWA: Paul Boissonneault and John Drew, Winter 1981-82.

DIEDRE III 5 5.9
The exact severity of this route depends entirely upon conditions. This is a steep, difficult mixed route involving some aid. It has seen few winter ascents. To the right of REMISSION by 135 feet is an obvious right facing corner with a birch tree at its top that begins halfway up the cliff. Climb up the "triple ledges" via short ice columns to a large belay ledge. Pitch two is very short and traverses right under a small roof onto another belay ledge below the dihedral. Pitch three climbs the dihedral and then a short pitch gains the huge terrace on the right via a gaint flake. The crescendo finish is the final pitch up the overhanging chimney/handcrack and steep face above. On the first ascent this pitch was sheathed in verglass and dripping with icicles.
FWA: Doug Madara and Tony Trocchi, Winter 1975-76.

JACK THE RIPPER I 5.11 or A3
FWA: Todd Swain, Winter 1980-81.

THE POSSESSED I 5.12 or A2
FWA: Ed Webster and Ken Nichols, February 1974.

To the right of these routes is an area called THE NORTH END, a very popular beginner/teaching area with a little something for everyone Approach along the summit road until just before it turns sharply uphill. The climbs are just in the woods on the left. A well used trail up a steep gully just right of the easy slab leads to the top of the flows which can all be top roped.

The most obvious climb here is a long, low-angle slab (grade 1-2) that is done in either one long, or two short pitches. Up and left of this climb is a steeper wall that usually has two flows on it, both about grade 2-3. They can be approached two ways. The first way is to do a pitch on the short wall below them (to the left of the main slab) which is grade 2-3 and often thin.. The other approach is to walk up a left-diagonalling ramp that begins at the base of the main slab.

In addition to these climbs, there are a number of short, steep pillars that form on a short wall about a hundred feet to the right of the main slab. They offer great practice on ice up to 80^0 and can easily be top roped.

THE UNICORN I 4 +
A steep ice corner and face located above THEY DIED LAUGHING, best approached by ascending the snow gully just right of the big easy slab at the North End and then following the trail along the top of the cliff. Rapel to start.
FA: Paul Boissonneault, Chris Noonan and Jeff Butterfield, January, 1978.

Cathedral Ledge
Upper Left Wall

A.	UNKNOWN	—	—
B.	ALPHA CORNER	—	—
C.	NUTCRACKER	5	106
D.	CHICKEN DELIGHT	5	106
E.	LAYTON'S ASCENT	—	—
F.	NOMAD CRACK	5+	106
G.	DOUBLE VEE	5	106

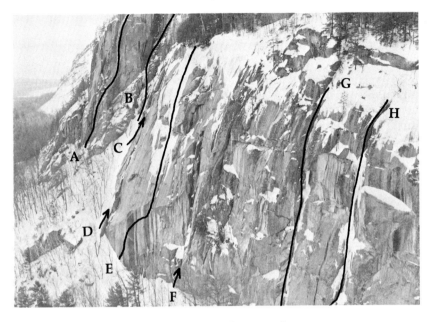

Cathedral Ledge
Central

HUMPHREY'S LEDGE

Humphrey's Ledge, 1.7 miles north of Cathedral and Whitehorse Ledges, is complex and has several areas of interest to ice climbers. Under optimum conditions, there are several ice flows on the main face; farther north, hidden around the corner, lies BLACK PUDDING GULLY, and farther yet are still more floes on the steep hillside. In addition there is a hidden practice area in the hollow up and left of the main face. Descriptions will begin here and continue north.

To reach Humphrey's Ledge continue north on West Side Road past the entrance to Cathedral and Whitehorse. Humphrey's main cliff will soon come into view straight ahead. Take care in parking on the road below the cliffs, and do not park at the Lady Blanche house on the right. The best descent from routes on the main cliff is by rappel, the bushwhacking can be horrendous. With two ropes rappel once to a two-bolt anchor 15 feet left of SOUL SURVIVOR (the birch tree to the right is weak) and then to the ground.

The routes in the vicinity of BLACK PUDDING GULLY are also easiest to descend by rappel.

HUMPHREY'S HOLLOW I 2-3
Hidden in the woods in the distinctive hollow to the left of Humphrey's main face is a good practice area that offers an uncrowded alternative to the more popular areas at Cathedral Ledge. Approach around the left side of the main cliff, walking for about fifteen minutes to reach the ice. Several moderate flows and a short, steep route characterize the area. Descend around the sides.

Farther up in the woods there is another route that ascends the obvious, broken, three-tiered cliff that forms the very back wall of the amphitheater. Contuning past the practice area for another fifteen minutes up a very steep hill will get you to the base of the bottom tier.

UNNAMED I 3+ 5.7
In the center of the cliff climb grade 2 ice for sixty feet to the first tree ledge, traverse right thirty feet or so and climb 5.7 rock (well protected) to the second tree ledge. A full pitch traverse (walking) will get you to the right-hand of two flows that ascend the third tier. Seventy feet of grade 3+ ice takes you to the

top. The left-hand flow is about a grade harder. Descend by rappel.
FA: Paul Boissonneault and Kevin Philibert, January, 1992.

THE MAIN FACE

THE SENATOR II 5
Southern exposure makes the formation of this climb a rare event. Since its first ascent it has never come into shape again. The route ascends a thin and poorly protected ice slab just left of the obvious dike that splits the main face.

The climb begins from a tree covered ledge that can be accessed by several routes, most easily the first right-facing corner of Soul Survivor. Two hard pitches lead to the top.
FA: Mark Richey and Rainsford Rouner, February, 1976.

SOUL SURVIVOR II 5
An ice climb of considerable stature involving a fine natural line and high technical difficulties. Pitons and a rack of Friends make the ascent easier.

The route follows the prominent dike that bisects the face. The first lead is an exercise in bridging in crampons up a right facing corner that leads to the right end of a large tree ledge. The second pitch, the crux, ascends the free-hanging column over the large overlap to thinly iced slabs above. Belay at a prominent white birch. Finish up a steep ice column in the dihedral above.
FWA: Kurt Winkler and Dennis Ellshon, January, 1982.

SUNNY SIDE OF THE STREET I 3
Climb the ice flow just to the right of the start of SOUL SURVIVOR for one pitch. When the ice suddenly ends at a seep, rappel off the route. An appropriate finish is needed to complete the ascent.
FA: Ed Webster and Butch Constantine, February, 1982.

WIESSNER ROUTE I 3 5.8
To the right of SOUL SURVIVOR by about a hundred feet is a huge left facing corner with a chimney in the back that runs the full height of the cliff. Two difficult pitches of chimneying gain the upper ice-choked groove. The rock climbing on this route will probably be harder that the ice.
FWA: Kurt Winkler

THE DESCENT CHIMNEY I 3 5.4
Ascend a thinly-iced 60 foot chimney at the extreme right-hand side of

Humphrey's.
FWA: Todd Swain, January, 1982.

HAGGIS SLAB I 2
The low angled ice slab to the right of the Descent Chimney.
FA: Todd Swain, January, 1982.

Continuing north past Humphrey's main face, West Side road curves to the left and in a couple of hundred yards a large broken cliff is seen high on the left. This cliff is home to two hard routes: BLACK PUDDING GULLY and TRIPECICLE. Both involve about a half hour's scramble through talus to reach their bases. Continuing north for about the next quarter mile is a rather featureless hillside characterized by short cliff bands and shattered buttresses. In a good year a number of climbs in the grade 2-4 range will be found here.

BLACK PUDDING GULLY LEFT II 4+
Seldom in shape. The line is completely separate from the main line of BLACK PUDDING GULLY. Climb the increasingly steep ribbon of ice left of the main gully for one pitch.
FA: Mark Whiton and David Belden (France), Februray, 1976.

BLACK PUDDING GULLY II 4+
The prominent ice-filled gully on the east face of Humphrey's Ledge. A two-pitch route, the first lead giving some extremely strenuous climbing up what is often a thin and candled vertical pillar. Finish diagonally right up a gully or to the left for a steeper ice flow. The best descent is to rappel the route from trees using two ropes.
FA: A.J. LaFleur, Rick Wilcox and Peter Cole made the first ascent in January, 1973, using etriers on the initial pillar. The climb has since been done without aid. Note: the first ascent party found the climb in unusually good condition (several feet thick) and it has never come in as well again.

TRIPECICLE II NEI 5
Ascends the ice slab and obvious icicle to the right of BLACK PUDDING GULLY. Two easy pitches up snow and ice slabs get you to the icicle's base. Climb a verglassed slab to the column and then strenuously up it to the belay at a hemlock tree at the base of a snowy chimney. Struggle up that to a ledge, traverse left under an overhang, and finish up a large ice-filled dihedral facing left.
FA: Mark Whiton and friends, Winter 1977.

Chris Dubé on the crux column on BLACK PUDDING GULLY at Humphrey's Ledge. Often thin and candled, this route is an exercise in control.

Photo by Peter Hovling

BARKING DOG ICICLE AREA

Extending for about a quarter of a mile past BLACK PUDDING GULLY is a series of brushy buttresses and short cliff bands that gradually diminish in height and culminate in a very prominent blue bulge behind the second house beyond the prominent roadside boulder. This bulge is THE BARKING DOG ICICLE.

Most of the climbs are in the 2-4 range, do not follow obvious lines and tend to go from tree to tree. Nonetheless there have been at least six routes put up here by the ever prolific Todd Swain and in his words "although short, this area makes for a good change from the North End (Cathedral), no crowds." It can be a really fun area to explore.

Perhaps the most significant hard route in the area is DOG TIRED (4+), the second major flow to the left of the obvious shallow cave (Pitman's Arch) a couple of hundred feet left of the BARKING DOG ICICLE. Steep icicles connected by very thinly iced walls make for a spectacular and dangerous route.

CEMETERY CLIFF

Continue north on West Side Rd. for about a half mile and there will be a steep hill with a rather brushy cliff up and left in the woods. Similar to the Barking Dog Icicle area, there are a number of somewhat nebulous routes on the cliff. Park along the road at the top of the first rise and head left into the woods. The two most obvious routes will be described below, though other possibilities exist.

BARNABUS COLUMN I 3+
The left side of the cliff has two distinct flows. BARNABUS COLUMN is on the left and begins directly between two hemlock trees. Climb a steep flow to a gully and the woods. Rappel off.
FA: Butch Constantine and Jim Tierny, Winter 1981-82, approached the upper part of the flow by traversing in from the left. In January, 1983, Todd Swain and Mike Hannon added a direct start.

DARK SHADOWS I 4 5.6
   The sister route to BARNABUS COLUMN climbs a thin ribbon on the left to below an overhang; traverse right and up on rock to join the former route. A knifeblade and #3 friend will be helpful.
FA : Todd Swain and Mike Hannon, January 26, 1983.

DUCK'S HEAD

   To reach the first area beyond the major clifs, drive about five miles north of North Conway on Rt. 16/302 and continue west to the intersection where Route 16 turns north in the village of Glen. Turn north and drive two miles to Jackson village. Directly opposite the covered bridge is a steep cliff on the west side of Rt. 16. This is DUCK'S HEAD. Park where you can and walk straight in to the cliff. The climbs are steep, and may involve some rock climbing depending on condition. Routes are described from right to left. Descend off to the right, or rappel.

WHEN LIGHT MEETS NIGHT I 4
   This is the last major flow on the right-hand side. The climb is one pitch long and usually thick.There are other short routes farther right.
FRA: Kurt Winkler, March 18, 1981.

LUNA GLACE I 3 +
   To the left of the previous climb is an ice flow in a right-facing corner. Poor ice and protection are characteristic, although a better winter may make thicker ice conditions than were present on the first ascent. It is suggested that pegs and a #2 Friend be carried.
FRA: Kurt Winkler and David Stone, on the night of March 24, 1981.

OVERLOAD I 5+
   On the left side of the crag is a steep wall that is typically encrusted with verglass. To call these next two routes ice climbs is somewhat misleading since most of the time the ice is thin enough to read a book through. Protection will be found to be purely psychological on these serious routes.
   OVERLOAD climbs the obvious central drip on this part of the wall. A hundred feet of extremely thin and technical climbing with little protection (pins needed) will finally get you to the safety of the trees.
FA: John Tremblay and Dave Rose, January, 1987.

THE LAMINATE I 5
The equally thin but shorter neighbor just to the left.
FA: *John Tremblay and Joe Lentini, January, 1987.*

EAGLE CLIFF

EAGLE'S GIFT I 5+
One of the more elusive routes in the region. Though frequently seen from the village of Glen as an inviting drip down the steep wall of Eagle Ledge, it is rarely in shape enough to climb. An extreme exercise in thin ice climbing.
Just west of the intersection of Routes 16 and 302 in Glen is a convenience store/Post Office on the south side of the road with a restaurant across the street. Just east of the restaurant. a dirt road heads north towards the obvious crag. Park where you can and hike in the dirt road. In a few hundred yards you will come to a gravel pit. From the very back and highest part of the pit follow an old overgrown logging road that leads towards the crag. Follow this for a couple of hundred yards then break left into the woods and head up to the cliff. The cliff consists of a steep wall on the left and a low angled slab on the right. Eagle's Gift is found high on the right end of the steep wall. Approach up a steep, brushy gully.
Sixty feet of verglass will get you to the heart-stopping drip above. On the first ascent, the climb's second pitch was about two feet wide, only a couple of inches thick and detached. After Winkler's lead there was not enough ice left to follow the pitch. Even in the best of condition the climb will be very technical and hard to protect. Bring pins and Friends.
FA: *Kurt Winkler with Joe Lentini and Alec Behr , January, 1985.*

IRON MOUNTAIN

Climbs on Iron Mountain are reached by turning north onto Jericho Rd., 0.8 miles west of the intersection of Routes 16 and 302 in Glen.

FRIENDSHIP ROUTE II 3
From Jerico Road take the first right on Glen Ledge Road following it through a chalet development. Follow this up and back left until almost level with an ice flow dropping off the side of Iron Mountain on your left. Bushwhack

along a red-blazed property boundary to a hill, then trend slightly left up this until the ice climb is visible through the trees. There are two pitches, the first thin, the second short.
FA: Kurt Winkler and Joe Perez, January 26, 1980.

MISGUIDED I 3

To the left of the former route by about 50 feet is a 60 foot flow. The first ascent was done in lean conditions; it may be a lot easier when thick.
FA: George Hurley and Marc Chauvin, December 18, 1982.

GIANT STAIRS CLIFF

ACROSS THE RIVER AND INTO THE TREES III 4

Follow the Jerico Road 4.4 miles to its plowed end in the Rocky Branch Wilderness. Hike for 2 1/2 miles to the Stairs Col Trail beyond the shelter. At the Giant Steps Cliffs, but below the actual col, bushwhack about 250 yards along the base of the lower cliff to its right-hand end. Depending on snow conditions, this approach could take three hours or more.The 125 foot icefall is climbed in two pitches. The initial section is thin and unprotectable. The steep and sustained finish, is considerably thicker. At the top, hike uphill 100 yards, then head down and right to a snow gully and the base of the route.
FA: Kurt Winkler and Joe Perez, January 6, 1980.

WHITE'S LEDGE

The next climb is located on the large cliff that forms the south face of Mt. Stanton. It is easily seen from Route 302 by looking north from a point on the highway just east of Attitash ski area. To get to the cliff, drive about two miles west on Route 302 from the intersection with Route 16 in Glen and turn right into a housing development called Birchview by the Saco. Take the first left and park off the road where it curves to the right. A dirt road goes straight ahead into the woods before the curve. Follow this until White's Ledge is visible through the trees on your right and then bushwhack uphill to the base. Allow about an hour in good conditions.

WHITE'S GULLY II 3+ 5.5

This route begins a couple of hundred feet uphill and left from the lowest toe of rock. Move up and right to a tree; then up straight before you traverse left to the gully proper (5.5). Follow the gully up and over a short vertical pillar. Two more pitches up the stepped ice flow above lead to the summit. The easiest descent is made by following the Mt. Stanton trail which leads east from the summit back down to the north end of the chalet development.
FA: Bill Kane and Kim Smith, February, 1978.

CAVE MOUNTAIN

STALACTITE II 3+

A short ice climb is found on the right-hand cliff of Cave Mountain north of Bartlett, N. H. Turn north at the main intersection in the center of Bartlett, (7.2 miles west of Glen), cross the Saco River, turn right and park at the end of the road opposite a farmhouse. The crag is clearly visible as a long broken rectangle and takes about a half hour to approach.

Climb a thin, detached ice curtain to ice bulges and a steep rock wall. Traverse left carefully until an exit can be made to the top. Number 2 and 3 Friends make the ascent easier. Rappel down a corner to the left of the route.
FA: Todd Swain and Jim Frangos, January, 1982.

HART'S LEDGE

The ledge, which is on the north side of the Saco River, is easily viewed from Rt. 302 a mile or so west of Bartlett village in the vicinity of the Silver Springs Campground. However, to reach it, you must turn north in the center of Bartlett (7.2 miles west of Glen), crossing the Saco River at a bridge. Turn west (left) and follow a road up the far bank of the Saco, crossing railroad tracks, and continuing along the river to a cluster of houses. Bear right, crossing the tracks again and aim right for the cliff. In a couple of hundred yards the dirt road will end and there is room to park. The cliff is composed of three distinct tiers culminating in a summit cap of orange granite. Due to its south-facing exposure, ice climbs at Hart's Ledge are seldom in shape, but in a good year there are at least six flows on the cliff.

HART OF THE MATTER II 3
A three-pitch route ascending the entire height of Hart's Ledge. The first pitch is up a moderately hard flow on the left side of the lowest tier. An easy ice slab follows in the center. The upper tier is climbed via an ice flow to the right of a prominent cleft on the right side of a large, rocky buttress.
FA: Brad White and friend, Winter 1977-78.

ICE TEARS II 4 +
A two pitch climb up steep ice on the lowest band of Hart's Ledge. Located in approximately the middle of the cliff. It is an excellent, steep route.
FA: Jim Dunn and Dick Cyrs, February, 1978.

CARDIAC CLIFF

This is a small south-facing crag located on the east side of the Saco River about a half mile north of Hart's Ledge. Drive in as for Hart's Ledge but at the cluster of houses after the first railroad crossing, instead of bearing right, continue paralleling the river past about five houses to the end of the road. Park and walk in almost due north, intersecting a logging road which is followed to the left to reach the crag. Allow about a half hour.

Though only a pitch high, this crag is densely packed with moderate routes and the location almost insures solitude. Due to its south-facing exposure, routes here never get that thick, or stay around for long. It is possible to get a brief glimpse of the crag from Route 302, and if you see white, then you'll know there is at least a skim of ice. The routes are all easily top roped and descent is around either side (easiest to the right). Routes will be described from left to right.

PACEMAKER I 2 or 4
The farthest left flow. Rappel off from an oak tree at mid-height, or continue on hard mixed ground.
FA: George Hurley and Todd Swain, January 22, 1983.

CORONARY BYPASS I 4-
The thin, detached runnel to the right of PACEMAKER. No protection for 100 feet.
FA: Todd Swain and George Hurley, January 22, 1983.

HARTLESS I 3-
The thickest flow in the center of the crag.
FA: George Hurley and Todd Swain, January 22, 1983.

CARDIAC ARETE I 3+
Another thin detached route; unfortunately there is no protection this time.
FA: Todd Swain and George Hurley, January 22, 1983.

EKG I 3
The last flow on the right. Thin and (you guessed it) poorly protected.
FA: George Hurley and Todd Swain, January 22, 1983.

EMERGENCEY ROOM I 1-2
The wide, easy flow above and to the right of the crag.
FA: Todd Swain and George Hurley, solo, January 22, 1983.

MT. TREMONT

CASPER THE FRIENDLY GHOST II 2
This obscure route is on an unnamed shoulder of Mt. Tremont on the south side of Route 302 across the river from Hart's Ledge. It is easily seen above a set of tourist cabins about 1 1/2 miles west of Bartlett village.
FA: Bryan Becker and George Stevens, Winter 1979-80.

SAWYER RIVER ROAD

XANADU FALLS II 3
An easy ice climb which makes a worthwhile route in lean snow years. Four and a half miles west of Bartlett and just after the bridge over the Sawyer River, the SaWYer River Road leaves to the south. Depending on whether there is logging activity in the area, the road may or may not be plowed. Drive, hike, ski, or snowshoe up Sawyer River Road for one mile to a house on the left. Across the river lies a large slab or scar on the slope above. XANADU FALLS follows an ice flow immediately right of this feature. Cross the river and follow a stream

bed, then a ridge to an open area. Bear right until the original stream bed is reached again. A large leaning oak tree marks the climb's start. After a fifty-five degree, thin, first pitch, four more rope lengths lead to the top. Descend the climb. About six hours, car to car .
FA: Kurt Winkler and Jim Tierney, January 22, 1980.

TECACO SLAB AREA

This sunny little area is found just south of Crawford Notch State Park and offers a variety of fun ice climbs from easy to hard. On bitterly cold days its sunny nature makes it a good alternative to the east and northeast facing climbs at Frankenstein. A little over six miles northwest of Bartlett is a large parking lot on the east side of the road, the trailhead for the Davis Path. To get to the main area, park here, cross the suspension bridge over the Saco River, and then follow the river upstream to reach the crags. The first area to be reached will be the Texaco Amphitheater, and a few hundred yards farther will be the obvious flow of the TEXACO SLAB itself.

Routes will be described as they would be encountered on the approach from the Davis Path.

THE TEXACO AMPHITHEATER
Several hundred yards to the south of the obvious TEXACO SLAB is a sheltered amphitheater with a number of short (100 feet) climbs that vary from grade 3-4 and are consistently thick and in shape each season. A sunny sheltered place to climb away from the crowds. Approach via the Davis Path bridge over the Saco River and bushwhack north for about a half hour. Only four routes will be described although there are several more possibilities.

THE DUNKING I 3
The right-hand end of the crag consists of three obvious routes on a steep wall. THE DUNKING is the farthest right, shortest route.
FRA: Most likely Todd Swain, Curt Robinson and Maxine Train, February 7, 1983.

THE IMPASS I 3+ 5.8
The central route about fifty feet left of the previous climb. Up a steep blue

column until blocked by a large roof. Traverse left around the roof to the top.
FRA: John Tremblay and Mark Arsenault, Winter 1984/85.

ANKLES AWAY I 3+
The next route to the left, ANKLES AWAY climbs up a steep curtain to a ledge and then easier terrain at the top. The name implies the flying style of the leader on a subsequent ascent.
FRA: A little sketchy, but probably Todd Swain, Curt Robinson and Maxine Train, February 7, 1983.

DOUBTING THOMAS I 4
On the left side of the cliff band, about 200 feet left of ANKLES AWAY is a 70 foot overhanging wall with several pillars that drip off it. DOUBTING THOMAS is on the right and climbs a steep smear until an exciting step right onto the free-standing pillar can be made.
To the left of this route are several other more moderate flows.
FRA: Tom Callaghan and Peter Lewis, February, 1986.

TEXACO SLAB I 2-3
This is the big blue flow that is easily seen directly across the river from a convenience store (it used to be a Texaco station; get it?). It is located several hundred yards upstream from the amphitheater, but can also be approached by crossing the river behind the store. If thick, several lines are possible, each being one long pitch.
FA: Dave Walters, Bill Ryan and Bill Adamson, Winter 1972-73.

EMBARGO I 2-3
To the left of the slab it is possible to piece together a line that runs for several pitches up and over a series of cliff bands ending in an obvious narrow gully on the extreme left end of the Missing Wall, the cliff above Texaco Slab.
FA: Unknown.

MOUNT BEMIS

Mt. Bemis is the rather lumpy looking mountain that lies to the west of Route 302 and is just south of Frankenstein Cliff. There are two areas here of interest to the ice climber. High on a shoulder directly across from the TEXACO SLAB are two wide, gentle flows that are harder to approach than to climb. Park near the general store and bushwhack straight in to the flows.

OPEC ICE FALL I 2
The left-hand of the two mysterious flows. Two or three pitches — which may not be worth the effort in a heavy snow year.
FA: Todd Swain and Jim Frangos, January 5, 1983.

GASOLINE ALLEY II 2 5.4
The easy mixed climb up the flow to the right.
FA: Todd Swain and Jim Frangos, January 5, 1983.

About a half mile farther north, just before entering Crawford Notch State Park, you will just be able to spot the top of a yellow icicle on a small isolated cliff on the northern-most hump of Mt. Bemis. Park as for Frankenstein Cliff. Walk south on the tracks for 15 minutes, then bushwhack up to the ice climbs. The approach from the tracks is steep and takes about 45 minutes. Routes will be described from right to left. Descent for all routes is easiest by rappel.

CYNICAL CIVILIAN I 3
The farthest right flow.
FA: George Hurley and Kurt Winkler, March 11, 1988.

DANCING AT THE RASCAL FAIR I 3+
The next flow to the left.
FA: Kurt Winkler and Peter Quesada, March 6, 1988.

ENTREPRENEUR I 4
This is the first route to the right of the obvious yellow pillar.
FA: Kurt Winkler and Peter Quesada, March 6, 1988.

VISION THING I 4+
Climbs the yellow pillar visible from the road.
FA: Kurt Winkler and George Hurley, March 11, 1988.

FRANKENSTEIN CLIFF

Location: Rt. 302, 20 miles northwest of N. Conway, NH.

Routes: Many routes, all grades.

Access: Park at base, walk RR tracks, ten minutes to 1/2 hour approach.

Descent: Many descent trails, easy.

Weather: *"Notch"*, lots of snow, see pg. 18.

Equipment: Standard ice rack.

Highlights: Incredible amount of ice, easy access, classics at all grades; *Chia, Pegasus, Standart Route, Fang, Dracula, Dropline.*

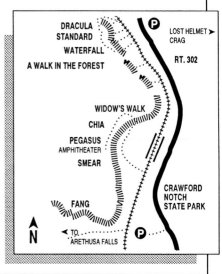

The varied terrain of Crawford Notch offers routes which encompass the full spectrum of ice climbing difficulties, from beginner's slabs on WILLEY'S SLIDE, to short, hard icefalls at Frankenstein Cliff. In addition, longer snow and ice routes are found on the south face of Mt. Willard and the west face of Mt. Webster. The latter offers climbs with up to 2,500 feet of vertical rise from the base of the notch to the summit and an equally long descent to follow. The setting in Crawford Notch, though not as alpine as you'll find on Cannon Cliff, is, nonetheless, a great area in which to climb. The routes are generally accessible and of high quality. Each different area will be described in the order in which they are visible when driving northwest from North Conway N.H. on Route 302.

No other ice climbing area receives as much winter traffic as Frankenstein Cliff, which has many excellent ice flows concentrated within a small area. Climbers of all abilities will find routes to their liking here. Most of the climbs are one to two pitches with simple descents through the woods. Drive north on

Route 302 out of North Conway for about twenty miles and take the first left a couple of hundred yards after entering Crawford Notch State Park A short road leads uphill to the site of the old Willey House Post Office now replaced with a private home. A parking lot is maintained by the state for hikers and climbers, but please respect the rights of the owners of the house at the end of the road by being courteous and by not blocking their driveway. All the climbs are approached by hiking north along the defunct railroad tracks.

The first routes described after Arethusa Falls are located on the Main Cliff, the tallest section of the crag, and the closest to the parking area.

ARETHUSA FALLS

ARETHUSA FALLS II 3-4

The long approach makes this a nice quiet place to climb. Park the same as for Frankenstein Cliff. The trail is marked and leaves the railroad tracks just a few feet left of the house. Hike along the Arethusa Falls Trail to a secluded amphitheater at the base of the falls. Allow about an hour in good trail conditions. All routes are up the center, but they can be dangerously unstable early in the season before the falls have completely frozen over. Many possibilities.
FA: Unknown.

FRANKENSTEIN CLIFF

FIRST ASCENT GULLY II 4

The farthest ice climb to the left at Frankenstein, up the steep ice gully in the back of a pronounced recess to the left of the Main Cliff. Approach as for the main cliff and continue traversing left from YOUNG FRANKENSTEIN for at least twenty minutes. The route received its name because three separate groups of climbers claimed the route as a first ascent within two years!
FA: Chris Noonan and Jeff Butterfield, Winter 1978.

YOUNG FRANKENSTEIN II 2-3

The route follows a right diagonally running gully to the left of SILVER HEELS, the farthest left continuous ice flow on the Main Cliff. The first pitch climbs an ice slab and rock corner to trees and the base of the gully. Easy mixed climbing and snow plodding lead to the top in two more pitches. Rappel the route.

FA: Todd Swain and Jim Frangos, January, 1982.

SILVER HEELS II 4

As with the other routes on this face, this steep and typically thin ice climb is rarely in shape. Climb the two pitch ice flow on the left margin of the face and rappel off.

FA.: Mark Richey and Alain Comeau, Winter 1977-78.

COCAINE II 4

Ascend the sustained ice flow just to the right of the former route. A two-pitch climb, it is rarely in good condition and seldom repeated.

F.A.: Peter Cole and Jay Wilson, February, 1978.

THE WRATH OF THE VALKYRIE III 4 + A3

A difficult ice flow with a short section of direct aid make this a stout undertaking. Climb steep ice to a blank rock wall and aid climb (passing a bolt) to the top.

FA: Franck Vernoy and Jack Hunt climbed the initial ice pillar in January of 1977. Stopped by a blank wall, it is unclear how they finished the route. On the second ascent, by John Drew, Todd Swain and Brad White in the winter of 1981, the blank wall was overcome by Drew who in desperation threw a cluster of pitons over the top which amazingly snagged in a birch tree. He then made a very scary jumar to the top.

THE SWORD AND THE STONE II 4 +

This is a slender ice ribbon about one hundred feet left of FANG, the largest ice fall on the south-facing Main Cliff.

FA: Jeff Butterfield and Chris Noonan, Winter 1978.

FANG III 4 +

One of the most spectacular ice climbs in the region, FANG is unmistakable when in shape, a wide stream of icicles that drip all the way down the main face. Rarely reaching all the way to the ground, the upper ice can sometimes be reached from the left. When in, the climb offers three very steep pitches of ice.

FA: Peter Cole and Alain Comeau, Winter 1977-78.

Bill Supple starts up FANG, one of Frankenstein's most spectacular lines. A series of icicles dripping down the length of the South Face, the route's sunny exposure makes it a rare visitor.

Photo by Todd Gregory

BRAGG-PHEASANT II 5

Perhaps the most ephemeral route on the face, it ascends a series of steep, thinly-iced corners to the right of FANG. The start offers poorly protected mixed climbing. Seldom repeated.
FA: John Bragg and Jeff Pheasant, January, 1974.

DIAMONDS AND RUST I 4 +

To the right of BRAGG-PHEASANT is a sheltered wall with four very short, steep, one-pitch ribbons of ice. Occasionally they are thick enough to climb. Ascend the sustained left-hand ice flow. Rappel off a convenient tree.
FA: Jim Dunn and Franck Vernoy, January, 1977.

CLOAK AND DAGGER I 4

Thin ice and a small overlap at twenty feet make this slender ribbon to the right of DIAMONDS AND RUST fairly unprotected.
FA: Todd Swain and Ed Webster, January, 1977.

THE SPACEMAN 1 4 +

Climb the second ribbon to the right of DIAMONDS AND RUST.
FA: Jim Dunn and Franck Vernoy, Winter 1977.

SHOOTING STAR I 3 +

After a difficult ice curtain, climb an easy dihedral and runnel to the top of the right-hand of the four flows.
FA: Ed Webster and Todd Swain, January, 1982.

Down in the woods below the previous four climbs are several short ice flows of varying difficulty. If you're on your way up to the DIAMONDS AND RUST area from a point before the trestle, and well left of The Amphitheater, you'll run across the following routes. Each route is eighty to one hundred feet high.

COSMONAUT I 3

The farthest left flow, fifty feet left of THE COSSACK and one hundred feet right of the left margin of this small cliff band. Climb steep ice to small trees, a bulge, and the woods.
FA: Todd Swain and Ed Keller, January, 1982.

THE COSSACK I 2

A large mass of ice lies hidden in the woods 150 feet right of the left-hand

end of the cliff band. Move up a slab to a steep bulge and the top.
FA: Todd Swain and Ed Keller, January, 1982.

WHITE RUSSIAN I 3
On the lowest cliff band, three hundred feet left of SMEAR, is a left-facing corner which fills with ice.
FA: Todd Swain, Dave Saball, and Brad White, January, 1982.

THE STEPPE I 1-2
Climb the left-diagonaling snow covered ramp one hundred feet left of SMEAR. The easiest approach to the BANSHEE or DIAMONDS AND RUST areas.
FA: Unknown.

RUSSIAN ROULETTE I 4
A mixed climb on the low cliff band two hundred feet left of SMEAR. Ascend a left-facing corner, past a chockstone at the bottom, to some ice bulges. Move over them to a snow slope capped by a final bulge.
FA: Paul Boissonneault and Todd Swain, January, 1982

During good ice years, several ice flows form on the slab immediately left of SMEAR, the large ice flow on the far left side of The Amphitheater. They are approached from the right starting up BANSHEE until a traverse left is possible on a big ledge.

SLIM PICKEN'S I 5
The flow farthest left of a rare ice area just left of SMEAR. One pitch of very delicate climbing up a lacy curtain.
FA: Kurt Winkler and Paul Boissoneault, 1982.

BROCKEN SPECTRE I 4 +
The thin ribbon of ice in the center of the slab features particularly delicate climbing with poor protection. Ascend up a verglassed slab to a stance, then climb the upper flow.
FA: Todd Swain and George Hurley, January, 1982.

WILD THING I 4
Ascends the small ice smear fifty feet left of BANSHEE. Begin just right of two trees growing against the cliff.
FA: Todd Swain and John Powell, January, 1982.

BANSHEE I 3

The smaller ice fall to the left of SMEAR. Depending on conditions, the first pitch is often mixed, but the upper lead is generally good ice.
FA: Alain Comeau and Jack Hunt, Winter 1977-78.

The Amphitheater at Frankenstein is best viewed from the train trestle encountered when walking north along the railroad tracks. It is highly recommended that climbers approach all areas within The Amphitheater via an easy access trail beginning at the south end of the trestle which leads directly to SMEAR and continues to the right. This will avoid the massive ice fall that regularly crashes down off WIDOW'S WALK. Six major frozen waterfalls descend from the rim of The Amphitheater with several minor routes as well.

SMEAR I 3-4

It is the left-hand flow in The Amphitheater. There are two ways to do the climb; the easiest is to overcome the initial bulge and climb the ramp on the left to a belay. Climb steep ice, then finish up easier slabs. A direct, and harder ascent (grade 4) forges up the vertical ice wall above the first bulge.
FA: John Bragg and Rick Wilcox, Winter 1972-73.

DOUBLE BARREL I 4+

Begin 75 feet right of SMEAR, up a detached, hanging curtain to traverse up and right to bush belay. Step left to the upper column and finish up bulges.
FA: Mark Grant and Dave Kelly, January 17, 1990.

BOW SAW BUTTRESS I 3-4

Climb the icy buttress between SMEAR and PEGASUS past bulges.
FA: Todd Swain and Dave Saball, January 6, 1981.

PEGASUS I 3.4

A beautiful and very popular ice climb, the wide flow in the back of The Amphitheater to the right of SMEAR. Once over the first bulge, climb lower-angled ice to the base of the final column. Climb this column (grade 4) to the top, or traverse right to a parallel column on the right. Up this to a ledge, then rock climb the wall above just left of a corner with a wide crack in the back. Wired nuts are helpful.
FA: Dennis Merritt and Sam Streibert, Winter 1970-71.

HOBBIT COULOIR I 4+

Climb the narrow and recessed couloir on the right side of PEGASUS to

a vertical corner filled with a bulging, awkward pillar. The vertical chandelier at the top is the crux of the route. An escape left onto PEGASUS is possible, in fact, the exit from HOBBIT COULOIR to the rock finish of PEGASUS makes an excellent and direct route.
FA: Bryan Becker, Winter 1978-79.

UN-NAMED I 4
This route ascends the right-hand wall of the Hobbit Couloir via a steep ice smear. Climb the first half of HOBBIT COULOIR until the ice can be reached on the right.
FRA: George Hurley and Vince Wilson, February, 27, 1986.

CHIA PET I 3 5.7
Climbs a narrow V-groove to the right of the former route. Begin up HOBBIT COULOIR until a mixed traverse right on a ledge can be made to reach the groove. Climb the groove up and over a chockstone near the top.
FRA: Charlie Townsend and Dave Auble, Winter 1989/90.

HARD RANE I 4
An excellent line that unfortunately doesn't form that consistently. When it does come in, belay just left of CHIA. Climb a very thin smear to a belay on a shelf, then head up and left on steep ground for two more short pitches.
FA: Dave Walters and Jeff Lea, February, 1979.

CHIA I 3 +
In the very back of The Amphitheater lies the large icefall, CHIA. It is easily identified by a distinctive ramp system running up on a diagonal from left to right. A moderate, and yet spectacular route, usually done in two short or one very long pitch. Chia was among the first plums picked upon discovery of Frankenstein in 1970.
FA: Sam Streibert and Dennis Merritt, Winter 1970-71.

CHIA DIRECT I 4 +
Climb a steep, strenuous curtain on the right side of the fall. Then cross-over the normal ramp system. Continue up the upper central columns.
F.A: Unknown.

THE CAVE ROUTE I 3
On the north side of The Amphitheater , this is the third icefall, counting in from the north side of the tressle. It's the short icefall on the left side of an

Ann Yardley on the steep start to CAVE ROUTE, one of a number of classic routes in The Amphitheater at Frankenstein.

Photo by Lee Stevens

overhanging wall with icicles hanging down off its lip. THE CAVE ROUTE, like its neighbor. WIDOW'S WALK, varies enormously in the amount of ice present; the greater the volume, the better the climbing possibilities become. *FA: Al Rubin and Oriel Sola-Costa, Winter 1970-71.*

WIDOW'S WALK I 5
Another route rarely in shape. When the icicles to the right of CAVE ROUTE touch the ground they offer a long pitch of very strenuous ice climbing with little chance of a rest on route. Be extremely wary when walking beneath this climb! It falls quite regularly.
FA: Alain Comeau and Jack Hunt, February, 1977.

THE BROWN RECLUSE I 5
Sixty feet right of WIDOW'S WALK climb thinly iced rock (pins needed) to an overhang. A strenuous pull on thin ice with marginal protection clears the roof and gains a thin smear to the top. A bold lead.
FA: Chris Rowins and Jim Surette, February, 1985.

BOB'S DELIGHT I 4
A sheltered, south-facing location makes this fine, one pitch route often the warmest in the area. The only drawback is that the ice tends to melt out from behind, creating hollow ice and potentially dangerous conditions. Nevertheless, it is very popular.
FA: Most likely John Drew, Winter 1970-71.

PRACTICE SLAB SOUTH I 1-2
Located on the left just beyond where the trestle ends and the tracks go through a narrow notch of rock, these ice slabs are an excellent area for top-roping and learning ice technique. It is a popular area in which climbers congregate. In years past it was also an exciting place to be when the freight trains came through! Rappel or descend off to the right.

There are several somewhat hidden ice flows in the woods just north of the trestle. Depending on the year and snow depth, a number of routes can be found here. For years these routes have had different, often contradictory route descriptions. Here, at last, we hope to set the record straight. These routes often provide a less crowded alternative to the more popular climbs nearby. An approach trail begins just beyond thePRACTICE SLAB SOUTH. The best descent for the following climbs is to turn left and climb back down through the woods to the left of LOST IN THE FOREST.

LOST IN THE FOREST I 2-3

This is the left-hand flow, a wide rectangular ice bulge about 50 feet high. In the past this was often mistaken for A WALK IN THE FOREST. A big snow year can virtually cover this climb.

FA: Most likely John Drew, Winter 1970-71.

A WALK IN THE FOREST I 3-4

This is the most obvious climb in the area, about a hundred feet right of LOST IN THE FOREST. It is a big wide flow about 100 feet high that is bordered on the left by a broken right-facing corner and becomes increasingly steeper as you go to the right. There is room here for several parties. Many have thought they were on MEAN MISS TREATER when climbing this flow. Sorry folks.

FA: Most likely John Drew, Winter 1970-71.

MEAN MISS TREATER I 4

Uncovered at last! This is the steep flow to the right of the former route and left of A CASE OF THE WILLEYS. It is not often in shape, but when it does come in offers a pitch of steep, thin ice. Rappel or descend off left around LOST IN THE FOREST.

FA: Unknown.

A CASE OF THE WILLEYS I 3-4

This is the farthest climb to the right before WATERFALL. It is a full pitch high and has an obvious ledge at mid height with an oak tree on it. Begin in a small corner facing left and follow an often thin flow to the top and rappel.

FRA: Todd Swain and John Mauzey, February 22, 1983.

Of historical interest is the origin of this famous saying,"a case of the Willeys". The Willey family were among the first setters of the area in the early 1800's. During several days of violent rain in August of 1826, a landslide swept down the east face of Mt. Willey. Hearing the roar of the slide and fearing their house would be demolished, the Willey family sprang from their dinner table and fled outside into the night. A search party would later find the bodies of Samuel Willey, Jr., his wife, two of their five children and two hired hands buried under the rubble. The other three children were never found. Incredibly, their home was virtually untouched, having been protected from the slide by a large boulder. And from inside the house came the howls of the only survivor, the family dog. Hence, "a case of the Willeys" a familiar phrase with a spine-tingling origin.

WATERFALL I 3

Located to the south of STANDARD ROUTE in a very secluded recess, it is one of the easiest and most ascended climbs at Frankenstein Cliff. The falls are visible from the railroad tracks, one pitch in height and usually rise in a series of steps. Descend around the left side or rappel the route with two ropes.

FA: Al Rubin and Oriel Sola-Costa, Winter 1970-71.

STANDARD ROUTE II 3 +

It is a given that there is a very real possibility of having to stand in line for this classic ice climb at Frankenstein. It is the longest moderate route on the cliff and comes into shape early each season. Walk north from the trestle for ten to fifteen minutes and you will not miss it, the massive frozen waterfall on the left with a belay cave at half height on the right. The normal ascent line climbs up the center to a belay in the right-hand cave (the left-hand cave partially collapsed several years ago and is now a semi-hanging belay). The second pitch steps out left and goes up a steep wall to bulges. Alternately you can often exit the cave via a bizarre window in the back on the right, joining the regular line above. A final long, moderate pitch over bulges gains the forest, or you can climb a final steep column.

FA: Sam Streibert and Dennis Merritt, Winter 1970-71.

STANDARD LEFT I 3

Climbs the independent flow that spills down the buttress just left of the left-hand cave. Two pitches to join the regular route on the right. Descend as for STANDARD ROUTE.

FA: Al Long and Al Rubin, Winter 1973-74.

THE PENGUIN II 4

An independent line between STANDARD and DROPLINE. Begin about one hundred feet right of STANDARD at a thin flow to the right of a buttress, up this on mixed ground to a tree below a bulge. The second pitch climbs the bulge and then continues up mixed ground aiming for a final column that is easily seen to the right of the top pitch of STANDARD. The last pitch takes the thin and steep column to the trees. (The final pitch can also be approached from the left after the second pitch of STANDARD.)

FA: Unknown, several parties may have done it in the late 1970's.

DROPLINE II 5

This dramatic icicle saw several attempts, including a spectacular fall,

before it was finally completed. The line couldn't be more obvious; the yellow icicle is up and to the right of STANDARD ROUTE. Work up steep slabs of ice, often very thin, below the main pillar and belay on the left in a small protected corner. The final exposed column, typically hollow at the start, is only a couple of feet thick and is vertical the entire way. Descend around DRACULA.
FA: Rainsford Rouner, Peter Cole, and Rick Wilcox, February, 1976.

LAST EXIT II 5

The improbable ice ribbon just to the right of DROPLINE. It has only been in shape on a couple of occasions, so has few ascents. Suffice it to say the seconds did not follow the leader on the first ascent.
FA: Rainsford Rouner, Winter 1978.

WELCOME TO THE MACHINE II 5

Ice on this route existed for only a very short time when it was first climbed, and it has rarely come into shape since. Long sections of vertical ice and an overhang make this one of the harder ascents in the region. Begin on the right side of the DROPLINE headwall forty feet right of LAST EXIT, and follow the thin line to the top.
FA: John Imbrie and Karen Messer, January, 1978.

THE COFFIN I 4+

An independent line that runs the height of the cliff between WELCOME TO THE MACHINE and DRACULA. There are two starts. To the right of the starts of DROPLINE and WELCOME TO THE MACHINE is a small buttress on the right, walk down and around the bottom of this to a shallow groove. Up the groove and over several steps to a belay on the highest ledge below the upper flow. Alternately, begin in the next groove to the right, about 80 feet left of DRACULA and just right of an overhang just off the ground. Pitch two climbs the steep flow to the top of the cliff (crux).
FRA: Todd Swain and Butch Constantine, February 11 (left), and 14 (right) , 1983.

DRACULA II 4+

Hidden in an acute, right-facing corner to the right of the previously mentioned routes. If STANDARD is the classic moderate climb, then DRAC-ULA is the classic hard route and can be ascended in a number of ways. The climb features three steep sections with resting ledges in between.

Most parties climb the first two steps in one long pitch, stemming on the second steep section to take some of the weight off your arms. Belay on a good

Kurt Winkler in full conditions on WELCOME TO THE MACHINE. Since the first ascent in 1978, this route has come into condition rarely and has had only a handful of ascents.
Photo by Lee Stevens

ledge on the left with a pine tree. The short final pitch climbs columns to an awkward bulge and the trees. Overhanging icicles often make this the crux of the route.
FA: John Bragg and A.J. LaFleur, Winter 1973.

DRACULA, RIGHT-HAND SIDE II 4-5
The right side of DRACULA offers a much more strenuous alternative, with thin ice and poor protection at the start. After overcoming a prolonged vertical curtain, a flared stemming corner offers some relief before the woods.
FA: Dale Bard and partner, Winter 1977.

THE HANGING GARDENS AREA
To the right of Dracula the cliff continues for a couple of hundred feet, curving uphill to form the right wall (coming down) of the obvious low-angle snow gully that is the common descent for all climbs north of Waterfall. This is home to a number of short routes that are easily top roped and is a good place to head if there is time left at the end of the day. The climbs range in difficulty from 3 to 5 with the hardest being a free hanging icicle that drips off an overhang near the bottom of the gully.

CLAWSICLE I 4
This climb forms a hundred feet or so right of DRACULA. It consists of a short, steep pillar that flows down out of a shallow bowl.
FRA: Kurt WInkler and George Hurley, Winter 1984-84.

WITHOUT REASON I 5+
This is one of the shortest routes of its grade in the area, and a testimony to the boldness of John Tremblay. Just as the cliff band begins to turn uphill to form the left wall of the descent gully, a large sloping ledge will be seen about fifteen feet above the ground with a large slanting overhang above it. Climb an ice smear on the right to reach the ledge, traverse left, and then swing onto the free-hanging icicle that drips down off the roof. Several pull-ups will get you high enough to tap your crampons into the bottom of the icicle, then climb strenuously to the top. Protection is poor, bring rock gear.
FA: John Tremblay and Pat Hackett, January, 1986.

SCRATCHING POST I 4+
To the rigth of WITHOUT REASON is a pillar. Stem off the rock (piton) to reach the free-standing column.
FRA: Kurt Winkler and Bruce Luetters, Winter 1983-84.

John Tremblay hangs out on the first ascent of WITHOUT REASON, a short and severe pitch near the north end of Frankenstein Cliff.

Photo by S. Peter Lewis

Uphill from SCRATCHING POST are a number of short routes that were all done in the late 1970's by Chris Hassig and friends. They range from 3-4 and are all easily top roped.

BEGINNER'S SLAB NORTH I 1-2
This is the final climb when walking north along the tracks. The slab is low-angled, providing good practice for leading or French technique.
FA: Unknown.

ANGEL CAKE I 5-
A severe, one-pitch, free-standing icicle on the Upper Tier of Frankenstein Cliff. Approach uphill above and right of CHIA.
FA: Jim Dunn and Franck Vernoy, January, 1977.

CHOCKSTONE CHIMNEY I 4
Climbs the left diagonaling chimney line on the Upper Tier to the left of ANGEL CAKE by a couple of hundred yards. After difficult and poorly protected mixed climbing, pass under a chockstone near the top.
FA: Jeff Butterfield and Chris Noonan, December, 1978.

FALLING ANGELSI 3-4
Just left of ANGEL CAKE begin on the right side of a small buttress, up thin slabs to a belay at trees above an overlap. Step left and climb a twenty foot column to slabs and the top.
FA: Alain Comeau and Kurt Winkler, January, 1986.

LOST HELMET CRAG

This is the short crag located high on the east side of the road directly opposite DRACULA. Park at a pull-out where the road crosses the Saco River and bushwhack up through the woods for about a half hour to reach the crag. A sunny exposure means that the following routes stand a good chance of falling off on a warm day. Descend by rappel or walk off. Climbs will be described from left to right.

THE SNUGCICLE I 2-3
On the left end of the crag is an ice flow capped by a squeeze chimney.
FRA: Todd Swain and Mike Hannon, February 15, 1983.

ROBOT LOGIC I 3+

To the right of THE SNUGCICLE and just left of the center of the crag is a steep icicle.

FRA: Kurt Winkler and Joe Perez, Winter 1982.

EXTENSOR I 4+

Right again is a route characterized by serious mixed climbing to a crux squeeze chimney filled with ice. Pegs helpful.

FRA: Kurt Winkler with Joe Perez, Winter 1982.

TAP TAP CRASH I 3+

The farthest right route on the crag. Up a thin, detached curtain to thicker ice and the top.

FRA: Kurt Winkler and Joe Perez attempted the thin curtain in 1982, but "it fell down" (with the leader) so they started to the left (5.4).Todd Swain and Mike Hannon did the first direct ascent on February 15, 1982.

Frankenstein Cliff
South Face

The Amphitheater — South

A.	WHITE RUSSIAN	3	135	F.	WILD THING	4	135
B.	RUSSIAN ROULETTE	4	135	G.	BANSHEE	3	136
C.	THE STEP	1-2	135	H.	SMEAR	3-4	136
D.	SLIM PICKENS	5-	135	I.	BOW SAW BUTTRESS	3-4	136
E.	BROCKEN SPECTRE	4+	135				

The Amphitheater — North

A.	PEGASUS	3-4	136	E.	CHIA DIRECT	4+	137
B.	HOBBIT COULOIR	4+	136	F.	THE CAVE ROUTE	3	137
C.	HARD RANE	4	137	G.	WIDOW'S WALK	5	139
D.	CHIA	3+	137	H.	BOB'S DELIGHT	4	139

Frankenstein Cliff
Standard Route Area

Frankenstein Cliff
Dracula

WEBSTER / WILLARD

Location:	Rt. 302, 25 miles northwest of N. Conway, NH.	
Routes:	Many routes, all grades.	
Access:	Park near base, 10 minutes to 1 hour approach.	
Descent:	Walk off, rappel or bushwhack, some very long.	
Weather:	*"Notch"*, lots of snow, wind. see pg. 18.	
Equipment:	Standard ice rack, some rock gear.	
Highlights:	Willard home of classic grade 2, *Cinema Gully*, plus shorter steeper routes, *Great Madness*. Webster has 2,500 ft. gullies, *Shoestring Gully, Central*. Mt. Willey home of *Willey's Slide*, incredibly popular.	

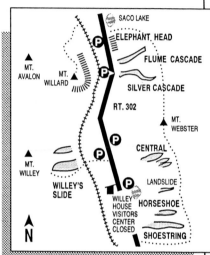

Five miles north of Frankenstein Cliff in Crawford Notch is a trio of mountains whose faces are virtually covered with ice each winter: Mt. Webster, famous for its alpine gullies that offer some of the longest climbs in the region,;Mt. Willey, home to perhaps the most often travelled route in the White Mountains, WILLEY'S SLIDE; and Mt. Willard, a complex face with classic climbs at every grade.

MOUNT WEBSTER

Mt. Webster's gullies, located on the face that rises above the east side of Route 302, while moderate in terms of sheer difficulty, involve an elevation gain of almost 2,500 feet, and therefore have an additional degree of seriousness attached to any ascent. Do not neglect to take into consideration the tiring descent and possibility for rapid weather changes when planning your itinerary. Park on Route 302 as close to the base of your intended gully as possible,

SHOESTRING GULLY, one of several long gullies on Mt. Webster that offer an alpine setting without the extreme weather of Mt. Washington or Katahdin.

Photo by David Stone

then head directly to it. The only obstacle in your way will be the Saco River. Fortunately, the river is only twenty feet wide at this point and fairly easy to cross.

For the descent, do not count on the Webster Cliff Trail, the safest way down, being packed out. The fastest way will probably be through the woods on either side of your gully and a swift glissade down the lower snow sections which will bring you back to the highway.

SHOESTRING GULLY III 2 (5.5 or grade 3 mixed for alternate finishes)

The southernmost ice gully on the massive west face of Mt. Webster. The lower section consists of low angle snow climbing, while the upper gully is considerably narrower, steeper, and usually full of ice, depending on how much snow has fallen. The normal finish is about six pitches long and takes an easy line up snow to the left. This is an excellent climb well worth the effort. In total, there is roughly 2,500 feet of approach and climbing from the road to the ridge at the top. Descend via the Webster Cliff Trail (if packed), or through the woods and brush off to the sides of the gully.

There are two other finishes possible: THE CHOCKSTONE EXIT (5.5) leaves the main gully on the right two pitches from the top ascending an obvious gully/chimney system; THE DIRECT FINISH (grade 3 mixed) takes a direct line up the final rock wall one pitch above the previous finish. Highly recommended.

FA: Original route—Unknown; The Chockstone Exit—Kurt Winkler and John Colebaugh, February 2, 1986; The Direct Finish—FRA: Alain Comeau, January 1986.

HORSESHOE GIULLY III 1-2

The next gully to the north of SHOESTRING GULLY, a few hundred feet to the left. Similar to its neighbor, but can be without any ice if there has been heavy snow.
FA: Unknown.

LANDSLIDE GULLY III 2-3

The long gully directly opposite the parking lot at the Willey House site and south of CENTRAL COULOIR by a few hundred yards. Typically a long snow climb.
FRA: Todd Swain and Ned Getchel, 1978.

CENTRAL COULOIR III 2-3 +

This gully with its many offshoots at the top is located about halfway up the notch somewhat south of Willey's Slide. Head through the woods in as direct as possible a line to the base. Although it is a typical snow couloir at the start, the section leading to the upper headwall provides moderate ice climbing.

The upper headwall is home to several finishes. The original finish is farthest left up steep icy rock to trees for one pitch. Descend through the woods or via the trail if packed out; either option is long.
FA: Unknown.

GREEN CHASM III 3 5.6
From the base of the upper headwall walk right 100 yards to a huge chasm. Two pitches of easy snow lead to a long mixed pitch and then another long pitch of ice. One short final pitch of easy ice leads to the trees. The trail is ten minutes up through the woods.
FA: Kurt Winkler and Peter Gamache, March 17, 1989.

HEART PALACE I 4-
The farthest right ice flow, on the upper headwall, 100 yards right of the GREEN CHASM. Climb up to an interesting cave and then up a pillar out right to easier ground above. It is easy to rappel the pitch with two ropes.
FA: Kurt Winkler Sunil Davidson, Drubha Hein and Shraddha Howard, March 10, 1990.

HALF BREED II 3 5.2
Can be climbed as a variation start to CENTRAL COULOIR or as a route in itself. In the middle of the large slab left of CENTRAL COULOIR is a long, thin runnel. Four pitches of thin ice, the first being mixed and the hardest, bring you to a point where it is possible to traverse right to CENTRAL COULOIR and either continue up that route, or descend.
FA: Jerry Handren and Sharon Hirsch, December 7, 1990.

FOOL'S PARADISE III 3
A long variation to CENTRAL COULOIR that begins several pitches up that route and looks for excitement by breaking left aiming for a large flow up high. After 4 pitches of iced-up rock, climb the flow for a full pitch through the woods to an exit crack and a further pitch of ice to the top.
FA: Tom Vinson and John Gospodarek, February 11, 1983.

NORTH SLABS II 1-2
On the northern end of the Webster Cliffs are several open, low-angled

slabs which occasionally ice up enough to be worth a climb.
FA: Unknown.

THE PILGRIMAGE II 3

The rock buttress at the extreme northern end of Webster Cliffs contains a narrow ice gully. What applies to other pilgrimages may apply here — the approach is the crux. Hike for about an hour up difficult scree to the base of the climb. After easy terrain at the start, climb a steeper ice gully over bulges to the top. Descend through the woods to the left (bushwhacking) or rappel.
FA: Mark Whiton, Winter 1978.

WILLEY'S SLIDE

Willey's Slide is one of the most visited ice climbing areas on the East Coast. It is located on the lower east face of Mount Willey and is easily seen from Route 302 about halfway up Crawford Notch. Just north of the Willey House site there are two dirt pull-outs, one on either side of the road. Look for a large boulder just into the woods on the west side of the road and you'll find the trailhead. Follow the beaten path up to the railroad tracks, take a right for a short distance along the tracks, then turn left and hike up to the slide. Since the slide is so heavily used, it should be obvious that safety precautions be observed; avoid climbing below other parties and always wear helmets.

WILLEY'S SLIDE II 2

Six or more full pitches of mixed snow and ice climbing can be done up this low-angled flow of superb ice. There are a multitude of moderate ice bulges and occasionally an ice cave near the top. After taking a moment to enjoy the marvelous view from the top, simply work your way down through the woods on either side back to the base. There is an additional small flow of similar angle down right in the woods which is worth a visit.
FA: Unknown

STREAMLINE II 2

This route and its neighbors climbs out of the ravine of Willey Brook, about a half a mile north of WILLEY'S SLIDE. Park as for Mt. Willard, and walk 300 yards south of CINEMA GULLY to a trestle. Walk up the right side of the stream for a quarter of a mile to a fork. Bear right and go 100 yards to a streambed on the left side of a rock slab. Follow this for many pitches.
FA: Kurt Winkler and Phyllis Austin, January 15, 1983.

FLAT FOOT FLOOGIE II 2+
   A two pitch route up the slab right of STREAMLINE. Begin in an icy corner and climb a hundred feet to a horizontal crack. One more pitch and rappel.
FA: Kurt Winkler and Phyllis Austin, February 8, 1986.

CANDLEPIN I 4
   A perfect grade 4 pillar in a hidden gully right of FLAT FOOT FLOOGIE.
FA: Kurt Winkler and Phyllis Austin, February 8, 1986.

MOUNT WILLARD

   The most extensive ice climbing locale in the north end of Crawford Notch is the south face of Mount Willard. In addition to the lower slabs, there are worthwhile short slabs and gullies to choose from on the upper face as well. One of the pleasant aspects of ice climbing here is, undoubtedly, the south-facing location which often makes for warm and comfortable climbing. But it can also be very windy.

   Parking for Willard is best found at the top of the notch at a plowed pull-out on the west. Walk south along the railroad tracks until beneath the lower slabs. If you intend to do a route on the Upper Wall only, approach via HITCHCOCK GULLY (2-3), the lower continuation of a prominent chimney system quite visible from the railroad tracks, or ascend a low-angle slab well to the north. To descend from the large tree covered terrace in the center of the face above all the lower routes, walk right until below the upper chimney of HITCHCOCK GULLY. Two short rappels, the first off an obvious white birch tree, or one long rappel will get you into the lower snow filled portion of HITCHCOCK GULLY which sometimes is an easy glissade to the tracks. If you complete a route all the way to the top of the face, bushwhack up towards the summit and you'll intercept a usually well-packed hiking trail which leads back down to the head of the notch and the cars. Routes will be described from left to right across the lower, then the upper face.

CORNIER DE LA MOUSE II 3+
   Located in a hidden buttress around the corner to the left of GULLY #1. Ascend a left-facing corner with mixed climbing, eventually exiting out right onto icy slabs. Two pitches.
FA: Chester Drieman and Todd Swain, January, 1981.

George Hurley on CINEMA GULLY, a classic route on Mount Willard and one of the most scenic climbs in the region.

Photo by David Stone

GULLY #1 II 4

The left-hand of three steep icefalls on the lower left side of the face. Approach via the snow gully below the right-hand gully (GREAT MADNESS) and traverse left along the cliff base to the start. The flow is somewhat narrow and can be done in one or two pitches. Descend around to the left to the base or rappel the route.

FA: A.J. LaFleur, John Bragg, and Peter Cole, January, 1974.

VARIATION: DIRECT START I 3

Below the approach snow gully is a slab that occasionally ices up to give a long, thin pitch as a direct start.

FA: Kurt WInkler .

VARIATION: GULLY # 1 1/2 I 4+

This variation climbs a steep V groove to the right GULLY # 1, and is harder than the main flow.

FA: Most likely Ken Andrasko circa 1977.

GULLY #2 II 3 + 5.7

Using the same approach as for GULLY #1, you'll find the start of this route. Hanging icicles dripping down an overhanging rock band mark the start. Avoid the icicles by beginning on the right and angling back left to reach the upper ice flow. The rock is harder than the ice on this one. If you climb directly up the ice on the left, the grade is NEI 4-.

FA: John Bragg and Peter Cole, February, 1974.

GULLY #2 1/2 II 3

Ascends the ice between GULLY #2 and GREAT MADNESS. Climb the long snow slope to the base of GREAT MADNESS. An easy pitch over ice bulges leads to a belay at a rock wall on the left. Move out left and climb through an awkward notch to easier ice slabs above.

FA: Todd Swain, Dick Peterson, and Brad White, December 7, 1980.

GREAT MADNESS II 5

The right most of the three ice flows is the most difficult. It is located about a hundred yards left of the base of CINEMA GULLY, the prominent central snow and ice gully. A short easy pitch leads to the base of a sustained vertical pillar, the crux. Climb strenuously to easier slabs and the tree-covered terrace.

FA: Jim Dunn and Dale Wilson, January, 1982.

FREEZE FRAME II 3 5.7

A mixed route up the face just to the left of CINEMA GULLY. The best approach is to start up CINEMA GULLY then move off left beneath its first ice bulge along a set of sloping, snow-covered ramps. Follow an obvious sloping ledge up to its right end, then aid off a bolt to slabs and a tree belay. Climb through trees to another belay at the base of an ice flow in a right-facing dihedral. Follow this to the tree-covered ledge.

FA: Todd Swain and Butch Constantine, January, 1982.

CINEMA GULLY II 2

This highly recommended climb ascends the beautiful wide open snow and ice gully in the center of Mt. Willard's lower slab, and is so named for an early cinematography project. Several pitches of moderate climbing lead to the large tree-covered terrace in the center of the face. The start of the route, while quite easy, is often quite thinly iced, and setting up secure belays can be difficult until you reach thicker ice higher on the climb. Nonetheless, it is a fine route. Once on the terrace, there are several options: descend around left of GULLY #1, walk right across the terrace and rappel down HITCHCOCK GULLY, or continue up any number of short climbs on the upper wall to the summit of Mt. Willard. The descent down HITCHCOCK GULLY is the fastest and easiest option however difficult it may sound.

FA: Unknown.

RIKKI-TIKKI-TAVI III 5-

Verglas and poor protection makes this an intimidating route which is not often in shape. Ascends the approximate line of the URSA MAJOR rock climb. Begin 200 feet right of CINEMA GULLY beneath the right end of a large iced overlap. With negligible protection, climb the ice smear up and over the overlap (the crux). Belay at an ice bulge on easy slabs. Continue up thin ice and snow to a belay bush on the right. Head straight up to a rock band after surmounting easy bulges. The last pitch moves right to a right-facing corner leading to the trees. It is suggested that you carry Friends in addition to short ice screws for protection.

FA: Todd Swain, Dave Saball and Brad White, January, 1982.

The following short routes are found on the upper east face of Mt. Willard. They are appropriate sequels to any of the previous climbs, or worthwhile done alone. To climb them on their own, there are two approaches: either up the lower portion of HITCHCOCK GULLY, or by climbing a low-angled slab well to the north of all the routes and traversing left. The only exception is CAULI-

FLOWER GULLY which is best approached by climbing one of the routes on the lower left face.

CAULIFLOWER GULLY I 2-3

This is the gully that is clearly visible from the road, curving around the left side of the large upper cliff directly above GULLY #1. A fantastic route that offers a logical finish to CINEMA GULLY or any route on the left side of the cliff. From the tree ledge above CINEMA GULLY traverse up and left for a couple of hundred yards through steep woods to reach the flow. Two pitches up the gully lead to the very summit of Mt. Willard. Descend down the Mt. Willard trail back to the parking lot at the top of the notch.
FA: Todd Swain and George Hurley, February 13, 1983.

EAST FACE SLAB I 3

Climb the large obvious ice slab immediately left of the upper chimney of HITCHCOCK GULLY. Similar in nature to CINEMA GULLY, it is another logical finish to that route.
FA: Unknown.

HITCHCOCK GULLY I 2-3

This is the most obvious, right diagonally running dike/gully ascending the entire height of the southeast face. It is quite impressive above the right end of the terrace. Spectacular climbing of a moderate nature makes this a very worthwhile adventure.
FA: Unknown.

EAST FACE SLAB RIGHT I 3

The moderate water ice flow to the right of HITCHCOCK GULLY. Very thick and reliable with several lines available.
FA: Unknown.

THE CLEFT I 2-3

To the right of the right-hand slabs is another obvious deeply cut gully. It is of similar difficulty to the upper portion of HITCHCOCK GULLY.
FA: Alain Comeau and Doug Madara, winter 1976-77.

THINKING OF JANET I 4+

After a thin vertical curtain, climb a steep sustained ice flow just to the right of THE CLEFT.
FA: Franck Vernoy and friend, Winter 1976-77.

LONG DISTANCE LOVE I 3
Climb the moderate pillar set back in a recess to the right of the former route.
FA: Franck Vernoy and Alain Comeau, Winter 1976-77.

DAMSEL IN DISTRESS I 4 5.7-8
On the far right side of an amphitheater, mixed climbing gains a short cascade of water ice.
FRA: Ed Webster, Susan Patenaude, and Todd Swain, Winter 1980-81.

READ BETWEEN THE LINES I 4
On the far right side of the upper cliff, look for an ice-choked chimney reminiscent of PINNACLE GULLY. Harder than it looks.
FA: Dougald McDonald and Chris Dube, January, 1987.

TRESTLE WALL I 3-4 mixed
This is the large road-cut crag on the Willard side of the tracks that is passed on the approach to any of the south face climbs. Just opposite a small trestle is a steep, broken crag that has some interesting mixed terrain. The most obvious lines are a short, right diagonalling, square-cut gully on the extreme right end that is about grade 3, and a zig-zag series of icicles on the far left end that is considerably harder.
FRA: Todd Swain and Jim Frangos, February 23, 1983.

Mount Willard — South Face

A. CORNIER DE LA...	3+	157	E. GREAT MADNESS	5	159
B. GULLY #1	4	159	F. FREEZE FRAME	3	160
C. GULLY #2	3+	159	G. CINEMA GULLY	2	160
D. GULLY # 2 1/2	3	159	H. RIKKI-TIKKI-TAVI	5-	160

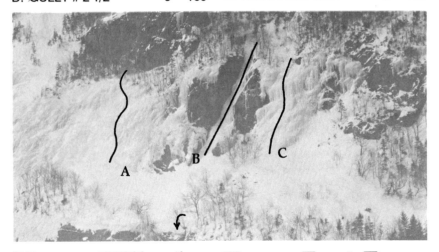

Mount Willard — Upper East Face

A. EAST FACE SLAB	3	161	C. EAST FACE SLAB RT.	3	161
B. HITCHCOCK GULLY	2-3	161			

More than two decades after its discovery as an ice climber's playground, the cliffs of Crawford Notch remain the Northeast's most popular ice cragging destinations. From slabs and gullies to free-hanging icicles, it can all be found here, and within minutes of the car. Here Dave Breashears takes on one of Frankenstein's most famous routes, DROPLINE.

Photo by S. Peter Lewis

ELEPHANT HEAD

At the very top of the notch is a small cliff that forms a natural replica of an elephant's head when viewed fromt the north. There are a number of climbs on the south side of the notch in the vicinity of this unique landmark, and they will now be described from north to south.

ELEPHANT HEAD GULLY I 3+
In the road cut at the head of Crawford Notch, directly south of the elephant's trunk, lies a one pitch ice fall. You couldn't ask for a shorter or an easier approach. This is a great route if you find yourself with an extra hour at the end of the day.
FA: Unknown.

In addition to ELEPHANT HEAD GULLY there are many other top-rope problems in the vicinity. The wall to the right of the main gully typically has several thin drips, and on the left side are some shorter problems which can be top roped. On the ELEPHANT HEAD itself a climb has been made right up the nose by Todd Swain at a grade of 5- on ice only a half inch thick. Though led on the first ascent, a top rope seems prudent unless you love to scare yourself. When climbing in the roadcut at the top of the notch please take extra care because any chunks of ice that you knock down can very easily land in the road.

THE FLUME I 1-3
Below the head of the notch by several hundred yards are two low-angled gullies just off the road. Both these frozen streams offer long practice climbs with difficulties up to grade 3. Descent is usually made in the woods to the south side of the gullies. THE FLUME is the upper flow.
FA: Unknown.

SILVER CASCADE I 1-3
The lower and more popular flow begins in an amphitheater and has two starts; up the main falls on the left or iced up slabs on the right. There is often an interesting ice cave that forms above the second pitch. About five pitches of climbing leads into a level area at the top just after a steep bulge, although there is more ice worth exploring on the stream-bed above.
FA: Unknown.

GOATBELL GULLY I 3+

This hidden gully begins about 300 yards south of SILVER CASCADE. Turn into the woods opposite where the Saco River meets the road and follow a deepening gully until it forks and becomes very deep and distinct. The left-hand fork is the climb, two pitches of moderate ice with a 35 foot 80 degree column at the top. Descend through the woods on either side.
FA:Todd Swain and Ed Keller, January 4, 1983.

MOUNT AVALON

Although the approach is sizable, the east face of Mt. Avalon offers several ice slabs of moderate dIifficulty. The climbs vary in length from those which are of bouldering size to flows of over 120 feet. Rappelling off is the quickest means of descent. To approach the area, find the Mt. Willard Trail and follow it for approximately one mile. Where the trail turns sharply left, one can get a clear
view of the flows on Mt. Avalon. A relatively straightforward bushwhack takes you in from that point. The flows are also just visible from the site of the Old Crawford House. They will be described from left to right.

PEER PRESSURE II 3

Trees divide the ice flows into three distinct sections. This route climbs the wide left-hand slab. The climbing is sustained.
FA: Todd Swain, Brad White, and Dave Saball, December 20, 1980.

MELLOW YELLOW II 3

The right section of the central ice flow is a yellow slab of moderate ice.
FA: Todd Swain, Dave Saball, and Brad White, December 20, 1980.

TALLY HO II 2

An easy route ascending the ice to the left of THE BATTLE OF THE BULGE.
FA: Todd Swain, December 20, 1980 .

THE BATTLE OF THE BULGE II 3

Located at the right end of the Mt. Avalon ice flows, this route has an obvious steep wall at its start.
FA: Todd Swain, Dave Saball, and Brad White, December 20, 1980.

MOUNT TOM

TOM'S DONUT I 4+

Hike in from the top of Crawford Notch along the Avalon Trail then bear right on the A-Z Trail continuing until a spur trail leads north to the summit of Mt. Tom. Look for an ice filled corner that leads to the top of a rock buttress; rappel.

FA: Bradley White and Jim Shimberg, Winter, 1986.

MOUNT WASHINGTON

Location: Pinkham Notch, Rt. 16, 20 miles north of N. Conway.

Routes: Grade 1-3 gullies, buttresses

Access: Huntington — 2.5 mile hike, other areas much longer.

Descent: Summer trails, easy gullies, exposed to weather.

Weather: Summit, **severe!** see p. 18.

Equipment: Many screws, rock gear, pins, 2 ropes, extra clothing.

Highlights: Classic alpine gullies, *Central, Odell's, Pinnacle*, plus mixed routes.

Warning: Sign out and sign in at AMC, worst weather in the world, *NO* facilities on the summit, back-country areas very remote.

GREAT GULF · AUTO ROAD · NELSON CRAG · HUNTINGTON RAVINE · ALPINE GARDEN · HARVARD CABIN · MT. WASHINGTON · PINKHAM NOTCH AMC VISITOR CENTER · LION HEAD TRAIL · TUCKERMAN RAVINE · HERMIT LAKE SHELTERS · LINK TRAIL · BOOTT SPUR · PINKHAM NOTCH AREAS · RT. 16 · N

Mount Washington (6,288 ft.) dominates the Presidential Range of the White Mountains, a massive bulk of rock whose summit is nearly 4,000 feet higher than the Appalachian Mountain Club Visitor Center at the base. It is the highest mountain in the northeastern United States. Mount Washington and the other peaks of the Presidential Range extend well above timberline. This region, covering several square miles, is rocky and windswept and has weather comparable with arctic regions far to the north.

Darby Field was the first white man to climb "Crystal Hill." He climbed the mountain, guided by two Indians, in 1642 hoping to find vast mineral resources. Though disappointing in terms of material riches, the history of Mount Washington is truly rich in terms of human triumph and adventure. From the 1920's the obvious challenge of the mountain's rugged terrain and harsh environment was a natural attraction. Throughout the generations, many people whose names are well recognized in the mountaineering world, Noel Odell, Robert Underhill, Bill House, Bradford Washburn, to mention a few, found adventure and inspiration on the flanks of Crystal Hill.

Up until the 1960's, Huntington Ravine was *the* place to ice climb in northern New England. Even today, the mountain's fearsome arctic weather is considered prime training for those preparing to go to the world's highest and coldest mountain ranges.

PINKHAM NOTCH

In the relative shelter to be found near the top of Pinkham Notch in the vicinity of the AMC Visitor Center are a number of short climbs that offer a more sensible alternative when the wind-chill is extreme on Mt. Washington.

GLEN ELLIS FALLS I 2+
Just before the height of land in Pinkham Notch, on the west side of the road, is a summer parking area for GLEN ELLIS FALLS. The parking lot may or may not be plowed; park at your own risk. Across the road from the parking lot, follow a trail to the bottom of the obvious falls. A long period of cold weather is neccessary for the falls to be climbed safely due to the tremendous volume of water that roars down behind the ice.
FRA: Todd Swain, Chris Taylor and Curt Robinson, 1979.

ICEMEN DON'T EAT QUICHE I 4-
Park at the GLEN ELLIS FALLS parking lot and head across the road aiming for the yellow flows that are high and slightly north. You will cross Lost Pond on the approach. The first pitch is moderate and ends on a ledge at 60 feet. Pitch two climbs the obvious yellow column.
FA: Unknown.

JACK FROST I 2-3
Climb the first pitch of the previous route then follow a low-angled gully up and left to a steep bulge and the woods.
FA: Todd Swain and John Mauzey, January 10, 1983.

ICE-CENTRIFICLE FORCE I 3+
Behind the GLEN ELLIS FALLS parking lot, up and right , is a mixed route that wanders up the steep hillside. Up a verglassed slab, left to a 25 foot pillar and then ferret out another 80 feet of mixed climbing to trees.
FA: Butch Constantine, January 9, 1983, with a direct finish by Todd Swain and John Mauzey the following day.

PINKHAM CASCADE I 2

Just south of the AMC Visitor Center at the height of land in Pinkham Notch is an obvious low-angled roadside flow that is great for practicing French technique.

FA: Unknown.

TUCKERMAN RAVINE

TUCKERMAN RAVINE II 1 - 4

Tuckerman Ravine is one of three major glacial cirques on Mt. Washington. Named for Prof. Edward Tuckerman, a noted botanist, Tuckerman Ravine is best known for its unparalled spring skiing. However, there are a few ice climbs in Tuckerman Ravine for the climber to enjoy, although singly none are of great significance. They are in best condition during lean snow years, or early in the season before the ravine begins to fill with snow. Begin the approach at the AMC Visitor Center at the top of Pinkham Notch, following the Tuckerman Ravine Trail for 2 1/2 miles into the ravine. Most routes wander up bulges on the main headwall for several pitches, either looking for, or avoiding difficulties. There are also some short flows near the base of Hillmans Highway, the obvious right-diagonalling snow gully above the AMC shelter and left of the headwall, as well as on the right side of the headwall above the summer trail. Descend either down the summer trail which skirts the north side of the headwall, or Hillmans Highway.

HUNTINGTON RAVINE

Huntington Ravine is the next cirque north of Tuckerman Ravine on the eastern flanks of Mt. Washington. Up until the 1960's, it was the focal point for almost all ice climbing activity in the region. With its 1,500 feet of elevation gain, exposed alpine setting and objective dangers from cornices, windslab conditions, and extreme weather, the ravine is never to be taken lightly. Its record of accidents, some of which befell very experienced mountaineers, clearly illustrates the dangers. More accidents have taken place here than at all the other ice climbing areas combined. It is clearly to the benefit of the climbing community that the U.S. Forest Service has two full-time snow rangers who check both Huntington and Tuckerman Ravine daily for possible dangerous snow conditions. Should conditions warrant, especially after heavy snow falls, they may post a warning advising climbers not to use the ravines.

The Appalachian Mountain Club's Pinkham Notch Visitor Center base camp is the headquarters for all winter activity on Mt. Washington. Information concerning weather forecasts, conditions on the mountain, and overnight space at the Harvard Mountaineering Club Cabin is available at Pinkham (telephone: 466-2727). It is particularly important that you register and sign-out at their front desk for your intended climb. When possible, stay with your proposed route and itinerary. This information will save the MRS time if you should need their assistance. Signing in is just as important when you return.

The Harvard Mountaineering club maintains the Harvard Cabin during the winter as a convenient base for climbers using the Huntington Ravine. It is located just east of the ravine on the snowcat trail leading up from the Tuckerman Ravine trail to the cirque. A user fee/reservation system is in effect at the cabin and one should arrange the details at Pinkham prior to hiking up. Capacity is limited as the cabin is small, but a certain amount of tent space is allowed in the immediate vicinity.

The approach to Huntington Ravine involves hiking up the first 1.7 miles of the Tuckerman Ravine Trail then turning right on an obvious fire road just a few hundred feet above the large bridge over the Cutler River. In a quarter of a mile the Harvard Cabin will be on your right. (Note: the Huntington Ravine summer trail leaves the Tuckerman Ravine trail on the right 1.3 miles from Pinkham; do not take it; it is not maintained for winter use.) After the Harvard Cabin, continue up the snowcat trail into the bowl at the base of the ravine. There is a litter and first aid cache here. Allow almost two hours to reach the first aid cache from Pinkham. Be conscientious and check weather and snow conditions before you leave the camp.

Several descents are possible once you've finished a route in Huntington and are standing on the Alpine Gardens. By far the most aesthetic descent is to traverse the gardens to the south reaching the cairns which mark the Lions Head Trail which is followed down to Hermit Lake at the base of Tuckerman Ravine, and then back down to Pinkham Notch. The assumption here is that the weather is fairly pleasant and there is no time pressure. However, if the weather is bad or rapidly deteriorating, you'll be looking for a quick way to drop down into the woods. Do so by hiking along the south rim of the ravine (if you've been climbing in PINNACLE, ODELL'S, or CENTRAL GULLY) until you pass the top of SOUTH GULLY and come upon the top of the ESCAPE HATCH (marked by a cairn). This shallow snow gully allows a hasty descent back to the bottom of Huntington Ravine during inclement weather. Use good judgement here since this gully has at times avalanched, and at times has been hard ice. Should you be climbing on the northern side of Huntington, walk right from the top of your gully until the rim begins to lose altitude, then scramble and bushwhack your way down easy terrain into the woods aiming for the first aid cache. Always carry a map of the region and a compass.

Few parties who spend the day climbing in Huntington Ravine ever make it a point to press on to the summit of Mt. Washington. There are **absolutely no open facilities** on the summit for shelter and the folks at the weather observatory don't like to be disturbed. A number of rescues have ensued as a result of "going for the summit" in bad conditions. Remember, if the weather worsens, do not hesitate to rappel back down your climb—your life is worth more than the amount of climbing gear you may leave.

THE ESCAPE HATCH I

The shallow snow gully on the far south side of Huntington Ravine, commonly used as the quickest descent route from the Alpine Gardens.

SOUTH GULLY I 1

The first major gully on the left-hand side of the Ravine. Several pitches of easy snow climbing with occasional ice make this a good, easy route. *FA: Unknown.*

ODELL'S GULLY II/III 2-3

Ascending the obvious and classic ice gully immediately left of the Pinnacle Buttress, ODELL'S GULLY is characterized by a large icefall which divides above into three separate flows. The middle is easiest, the left somewhat harder, and the right is the most difficult. In bad weather, locate a ramp at the top of the left flow which descends to the bowl near the base of SOUTH GULLY.
FA: Noel E. Odell, Lincoln O'Brien, J.C. Hurd and Robert L.M. Underhill, March 16, 1928.

PINNACLE GULLY III 3

One of the most aesthetic ice gullies in New England, this is the narrow gully between Pinnacle Buttress and Central Buttress. The first pitch, generally considered to be the crux of the route, consists of sustained sixty degree ice. The remainder of the gully is somewhat easier, with several more pitches of moderate snow and ice.
FA: Samuel A Scoville and Julian Whittlesey, February 8, 1930.

Perhaps New Englands' most beautiful gully climb, PINNACLE GULLY ascends an uncompromising line up a deep cleft in Huntington Ravine.

Photo by Ed Webster

CLOUDWALKER II 4 5.7

A mixed route following the summer line of a climb by the same name up the massive buttress left of CENTRAL GULLY. Just above the start of CENTRAL GULLY, climb an iced crack on the left to a thin smear, and then more ice to a crack out left below a roof.

FA: Chris Dube and Bill Holland, January, 1989.

LEFT WALL OF CENTRAL GULLY II 2

This short variation climbs the wall to the left of CENTRAL GULLY a couple of hundred feet below the top of that route.

FA: Alan Wilcox and William P. House, March, 1934.

CENTRAL GULLY I 1

Bordering the wall of the Central Buttress, this prominent snow laden gully was the first winter route in Huntington Ravine. It is one of the longest climbs in the ravine. Begin at the top of The Fan just to the right of the base of PINNACLE GULLY. After one or two leads of low angle ice climbing, several more pitches of straight forward snow climbing lead to the Alpine Gardens. An immense cairn marks the top of the climb.

FA: A.J. Holden and N.L. Goodrich, February 23, 1927.

DIAGONAL II 2

To the right of CENTRAL GULLY, hidden behind a rock buttress, is a gully running diagonally left. The bottom ice slabs of YALE GULLY must be ascended to reach this gully's base. Once there, an easy snow gully leads to the rim of the ravine.

FA: Unknown.

YALE GULLY II 2.3

After taking any of several routes up the lower ice slabs directly in the center of the ravine, YALE GULLY follows a slightly right-leaning shallow gully to the lip. A long, varied and enjoyable route. The assorted variations at the start are all about the same difficulty.

FA: Unknown.

DAMNATION BUTTRESS II 3

The broken buttress to the right of YALE GULLY is a surprisingly good mixed route. Take a line directly up the middle of the buttress following the line of least resistance.

FA: Unknown.

DAMNATION GULLY III 3

A classic gully climb, the left of two deeply cut gullies on the north side of Huntington Ravine. Two short ice bulges add spice to what is otherwise a predominantly snow-filled gully. Occasionally a cornice forms on the rim, but it is easily avoided. DAMNATION is the longest climb in the ravine.
FA: William L. Putnam and Andrew J. Kaufman, January 31, 1943.

NORTH GULLY II 3

Ascends the most north gully in the ravine, Just to the right of DAMNATION GULLY. Move up the lower snow gully to where DAMNATION and NORTH GULLIES fork. After a steep ice bulge, the remainder of the route is mixed snow and ice and quite pleasant.
FA: Maynard M. Miller and William Latady, December, 1942.

THE GREAT GULF

The quickest approach (though all are long) is via the Osgood Trail from the Glen House, then along the Great Gulf Trail into Spaulding Lake. The distance is 6.2 miles. The Gulf can also be approached by climbing up the Tuckerman Ravine trail and then dropping down the other side, but this makes for an incredibly hard day, in essence climbing Mt. Washington twice. However you choose to get there, climbs in the Great Gulf, even though moderate technically, are very serious given the long delay in getting rescuers to the scene of any accident. Bivouac equipment and self-rescue capabilities are essential.

GREAT GULF HEADWALL III 1-2

Ascends the headwall of the large cirque, the Great Gulf, on the north side of Mt. Washington. In lean snow years a considerable amount of water ice will be found on the flanks of this 1,000 foot headwall. A long approach, no matter which route you choose.
FA: Unknown.

WAIT UNTIL DARK GULLY III 3

Not visible from Spaulding Lake, WAIT UNTIL DARK GULLY is the most prominent fault line up the right side of the Great Gulf. It ends just beneath the summit of Mt. Clay. At the start, stay to the left up a series of ice bulges. Above, follow a moderate snow and ice gully, with some danger from snow slides, to its top . Hike up to the Cog Railway, the summit, and then return down the Auto Road .

FA: Kurt Winkler and Jim Tierney, February, 1981. Climbed during a lean snow year, the round trip took fourteen hours car to car.

MADISON GULF

The following selection of routes is located in the peaceful setting of Madison Gulf, situated between the east face of Mt. Adams and the south ridge (the Osgood Ridge) of Madison. Six or more flows grace the Madison Gulf Headwall in winter and offer a secluded alternative to the often crowded atmosphere of Huntington Ravine. Approach from the Glen House via the Osgood Trail. Follow the Madison Gulf Cut-off to the Madison Gulf Trail and the bottom of the gulf. The hike is roughly four miles long and has been described as "horrendous". Best done during lean snow years. As with routes in the Great Gulf, climbing in this area should be approached with an extra measure of caution since rescue is potentially many hours away. Routes will be described in relation to the central route, POINT, first left, then right.

POINT II 3+
The massive central ice flow just left of a rock rib which splits the ice. Two leads up moderate ice lead to the crux third pitch, which boasts a short, vertical headwall. One final lead gets you up to the top. Descend on rappel from tree anchors on the climb's left side.
FA: Matt Peer and Alec Behr, February 4, 1980.

POINTLESS 1 3+
One hundred feet left of POINT is a one pitch slab capped by a 15 foot 80 degree column. Descend by rapell or bushwhack around left (facing cliff).
FA: Todd Swain, solo, December 21, 1982.

POINT OF NO RETURN I 4
Continue left another couple of hundred feet to the next major flow. Climb moderate ice for two pitches to two prominent vertical columns; climb one of the two to the top, reminiscent of PEGASUS.
FA: Todd Swain, solo, December 21, 1982.

POINTILLISM I 2-3
Left of POINT OF NO RETURN by another hundred feet climb up low

angled slabs to a steep little column and the woods. Descend left.
FA: Todd Swain, solo, December 21, 1982.

COUNTERPOINT II 4
The right side of the large ice flow is considerably harder. After one lead of moderate ice, climb two more pitches with some vertical ice. Descend as for the previous climb.
FA: Matt Peer and Alec Behr, February 4, 1980.

KING RAVINE

The King Ravine is located on the northern side of Mt. Adams. As for this and other cirques in the Presidential Range, it takes a fairly light snow year for any of the underlying ice to be exposed on the routes. During normal to heavy snow winters, don't expect much ice. However, you will be guaranteed of a long walk in, especially if the trails aren't tracked. Start the approach at the Ravine House Site parking lot (the sign may say "Appalachia") on Route 2 in Randolph approximately six miles from Gorham, N.H. Begin the hike on the Airline Trail, to the Short Line, joining the Randolph Path for a mile or so, and then continuing on the Short Line Trail to the bottom of the Ravine (not as complicated as it sounds). This is yet another isolated area to climb in, although, unlike the Great Gulf and the Madison Gulf, help in an emergency is readily at hand at Grey Knob, a Randolph Mountaineering Club cabin at timberline near the western rim of King Ravine. It is staffed all winter and is reached by the Randolph Path from the base of the ravine.

KING RAVINE HEADWALL III 1-2
Most winter ascents follow the summer trail up The Headwall. Once you emerge from The Gateway, probably the best descent will be to cross over to Madison Springs Hut and return to the road by the Valley Way Trail .
FA: Unknown.

GREAT GULLY III 1-2
On the right-hand side of the King Ravine Headwall lies the GREAT GULLY. This long snow and ice gully reaches the lip of the King Ravine Headwall just below Thunderstorm Junction. Descend via the trail to Crag Camp, and the the Spur Link to the Randolph Path. Beware of avalanches on this wide open gully.
FA:Unknown.

P.F. FLYER II/III 3-4

To the right of Great Gully lies another gully that is hard to see and even harder to approach but is well worth the effort. Four pitches of moderate climbing to an escape left or harder mixed finish straight up.

FRA: Paul Flannegan, George and Peter Wallace, Winter 1976/77.

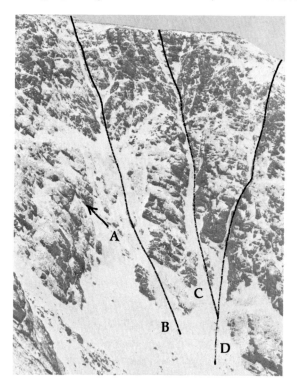

Huntington Ravine North

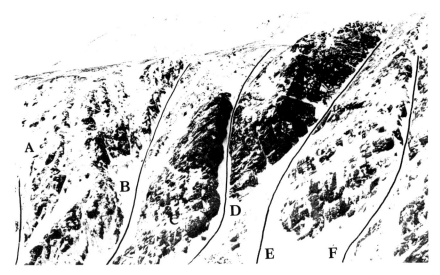

Huntington Ravine — South

A. SOUTH GULLY	1	172	D. PINNACLE GULLY	3	172
B. ODELL'S GULLY	2-3	172	E. CENTRAL GULLY	1	174
C. PINNACLE BUTTRESS			F. DIAGONAL	2	174

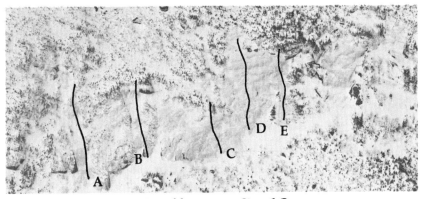

Madison Gulf

A. POINTILISM	2-3	176	D. POINT	3+	176
B. POINT OF NO RETURN	4	176	E. COUNTERPOINT	4	177
C. POINTLESS	3+	176			

EVANS NOTCH

Location: Rt. 113, 45 minutes from N. Conway, NH.

Routes: Grades 2-4, high concentration at several areas.

Access: Basin, Shell Pond—20 minutes. East Royce, 3 mile ski.

Descent: From bushwhack, to rapell, to easy walk, depends on the area.

Weather: *"Notch"*, see pg. 18.

Equipment: Standard ice rack, some rock gear.

Highlights: Very secluded, Shell Pond has many routes in small area. East Royce has potential for more hard routes.

Warning: *Very* isolated, be self-sufficient.

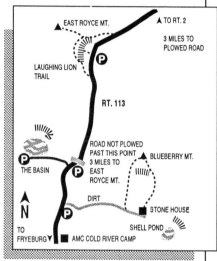

Evans Notch is a beautiful and isolated spot straddling the Maine and New Hampshire border just east of Mt. Washington. It is reached via Route 2 and 113 from the north and Route 113 from Fryeburg, Maine, from the south.

Truly "off the beaten path," the history of climbing in the notch is a bit sketchy. In the mid 1970's Tom Lyman climbed in the area, but his routes were not recorded. In 1976 Doug Burnell saw the cliffs while on a snowmobile trip with his father and began to explore the area, doing a number of routes, primarily with Doug Tescher. In the early 1980's Kurt Winkler made several trips with various partners cleaning up many of the remaining lines. Since then the area has been visited periodically, though new route information has been slow in appearing, and descriptions have been confusing at best.

The road through the notch is closed during the winter so the approach calls for an uphill ski or snowshoe of about 3 miles in either direction. Heading north, the main flows are seen on the left along the east face of East Royce

Mountain. They are surrounded by trees and vegetation, but are generally steep and between 1 and 3 pitches in length. The trip, either on skis or snowshoes, and the quiet, uncrowded atmosphere make it a worthwhile destination. The routes in Evans Notch will be described from south to north beginning at Shell Pond and continuing to the main area on East Royce Mt.

SHELL POND

Described as a "mini-Frankenstein," Shell Pond is an excellent area with many possibilities and is sure to be far from the crowds. It is reached via a dirt road, Shell Pond Rd., that heads east 0.7 miles north of the AMC's Cold River Camp on Rt. 113. This is just south of The Basin at the entrance to Evans Notch. How far you will be able to drive on Shell Pond Rd. is dependent on road conditions. The road is on private property and every courtesy should be given to the landowners. If the road is plowed, drive 1.1 miles to a gate just a few hundred yards before a stone house. Please avoid walking through the yard by using fields to the south.

Just past the house a snowmobile trail will lead east in the direction of the obvious cliffs. In just a couple of minutes a bridge will be crossed and soon you will reach the cliffs. This is a complex area and a little exploring will reveal a multitude of routes. A favorite "secret" area for years, accurate first ascent information is hard to confirm, although Bob Parrot, Jeff Butterfield, Randy Rackcliff, Steve Damboise and others have climbed here.

The first cliff reached will be a 40 foot vertical wall on the left that is about a hundred feet long and has many top rope problems in the grade 4-5 range. Further east and uphill is a larger cliff. On the left end of this cliff is an easy slab that is climbed for a pitch and then finishes up a short, steep, grade 3 step. To the right and around a buttress is a beautiful 60 foot grade 5 column in a corner. Rock pro will be helpful for this one.

Continuing on the snowmobile trail a 70 foot wall will be found to the south with an obvious 5.4 chimney on its left side. The main wall is grade 4. This cliff is easily seen from the end of the dirt road.

Farther along the trail, climb over a shoulder to reach more climbs in the woods. From left to right find a 100 foot grade 4-, a 50 foot grade 4, a full pitch grade 3 and a short, 40 foot grade 5 pillar. In addition to these areas there is a huge cliff up and right of the rest that is reported to be home to a very spectacular route that has yet to come into shape. This and many other possibilities abound for those willing to explore.

BLUEBERRY MOUNTAIN

Just before reaching the stone house on the Shell Pond Rd. you will see two trails on the north, the White Cairn Blueberry Ridge Trail, and the Stone House Trail; both lead to the summit of Blueberry Mt. Below the summit on the south side is a 180 foot ledge with at least two flows on it, a thick grade 3 on the left, and a grade 3-4 chimney on the right. The approach takes about an hour and is usually unpacked.

THE BASIN

BUBBLE GULLY II 3+
Just after the official entrance to Evans Notch, turn west at signs for The Basin. Park in a parking lot and walk across the frozen lake to a cliff on the right. At the crag's left end, and hidden around a corner, is a narrow 150 ft. gully. Climb the gully in two leads. The second lead is steep and short.
FA: Kurt Winkler and Joe Perez, February 17, 1980.

UNKNOWN II 3
This is the obvious diagonalling gully visible from The Basin. It is several hundred yards left of BUBBLE GULLY. The flow is characterized by two obvious tiers, the first being the hardest.
FRA: Bob Parrott and Barry Rugo, January, 1992.

COLLARBONE GULLY I 3
A short distance north of the entrance to The Basin is an obvious red brick house just off the road on the right. Behind the house and slightly north is a small crag on the east side of the road. COLLARBONE GULLY follows a narrow slot on the cliff's right side with an overhanging wall above. The route has been described as a "mini-PINNACLE GULLY" by the first ascentionists.
FA: Bob Parrot and Dave Lattimer, early 1980's.

EAST ROYCE MOUNTAIN

This is the major climbing area in Evans Notch. Route 113 runs through the notch but is not plowed in the winter. Park either at The Basin (on the south) or at the junction with Route 2 (on the north). The approach from either end is about three miles long and is easily skied. The climbs are all found on the east face of East Royce mountain amidst a jumble of cliff bands and tree ledges and can be identified from the road. Descents can be difficult, be prepared to rappel or bushwhack. The isolated location of this area means rescuers will be long in coming, so bring extra equipment (sleeping bags, stoves etc.) and food and be sure someone is aware of your itinerary.

RIGHTS OF SPRING II 4 5.6

This route ascends the left side of the lower Main Face. The major feature is a large right facing corner near the top, with a curtain of ice to its right. The first pitch climbs an ice flow below the corner to a tree belay on the left. Move out right from here to the first major ice flow. A huge icicle will be seen in the major dihedral above. The third pitch starts with thirty feet of mixed climbing to reach solid ice. A steep column on the final wall leads to the finish. To descend, first hike up and left to a mineral boulder, then down and left through a valley until you reach the Laughing Lion Trail. Follow this to a beaver pond, then crash through the brush to the car. An alternate descent traverses right to a snow slope where a series of low-angled rappels will bring you to the bottom in the vicinity of EXIT STAGE LEFT.
FA: Kurt Winkler and Joe Perez, February 21, 1980.

CALIFORNIA KID I 4-

After an initial vertical section of 15 ft., the flow eases to a series of steep steps with a few thin spots. Belay at trees above and rappel.
FA: Bill Kane, John Bragg, and Rick Hatch, December 30, 1981.

WHEN FRIGHT MEETS MIGHT I 4+

A logical finish to CALIFORNIA KID climbing the central pillar on the curtained wall above (just right of the last pitch of RIGHTS OF SPRING). Two pitches, the first with poor protection, the second traversing left under an overhang to steep ice, get you to the top. Descend as for RIGHTS OF SPRING.
FA: Todd Swain, Kurt Winkler and George Hurley, January 7, 1983.

OPENING NIGHT JITTERS I 4

A one pitch route that begins just left of EXIT STAGE LEFT climbing a steep curtain and then lower-angled ice to trees. Rappel.

FA: Brad White, Doug Burnell and Mike Brady, Winter, 1978.

BALCONY SEAT II 4

This route continues the line of OPENING NIGHT JITTERS all the way to the top of the cliff and finishes up a steep flow just to the right of WHEN FRIGHT MEETS MIGHT. Descend right and rappel.

FA: George Hurley and Marc Chauvin.

EXIT STAGE LEFT I 4+

To the right of BALCONY SEAT is a steep runnel which leads to lower angled slabs above. This and the following three routes are easy to rappel.

FA: Kurt Winkler, February 10, 1982.

CURTAIN CALL I 4

An excellent icicle climb to the right of EXIT STAGE LEFT, complete with a steep column and layback moves. The crux is getting established on the icicles at the start.

FA: Kurt Winkler and Jim Tierny, February 10, 1980.

EXIT STAGE RIGHT I 3

The slightly easier curtain just right of CURTAIN CALL.

FA: Kurt Winkler, Todd Swain and George Hurley, January 7, 1983.

PROMPTER'S BOX I 2

Climb the hidden gully 100 feet right of CURTAIN CALL. A curtain leads to a ramp and the top.

FA: George Hurley, Todd Swain and Kurt Winkler, January 7, 1983.

THREE'S COMPANY II 4

The route climbs the left side of the PILGRIM'S PROGRESS trio of ice flows. Stay generally left the entire way. After a pitch up steep bulges to a tree belay, climb mixed snow and more ice bulges to another tree. Pitch three is the crux: ascend a thinly iced slab to an alcove below an ice curtain barrier. Finish up the second set of icicles from the left.

FA: Kurt Winkler, Joe Perez, and Phil Ostrosky, February 24, 1980.

Kurt Winkler starts up the initial curtain of EXIT STAGE RIGHT on the first ascent.
Photo by Todd Swain

PILGRIM'S PROGRESS III 4

The route is a long collection of pitches and flows. Attention to directions here will make locating the route easier. Looking at the main cliff from the road, there is an intrusion of light-colored rock shaped like a pitchfork in the top-most sheer cliff. Under this, rising from the ground, is a heart-shaped series of ice falls that are joined at their base and top. At the start of the flows is a hidden flow that branches off right. This is PILGRIM'S PROGRESS. Climb two bulges and belay after a full pitch. Another long pitch follows easy ice up and left to more bulges and a tree belay on the right.

Walk up and right into the woods about 200 yards to a large rock overhang. Bypass this by walking further right up to and around a distinctive prow of rock to another ice fall. (This is easily visible from the road as the upper ice flow below and to the right of the "pitchfork" face.) Climb a short pitch up bulges to the right of a vertical icicle to a flat area and belay.

The crux climbs the long ice flow above to the trees. Descend by going left at the top of the climb and through trees, down ramps and hills, to the tree buttress that forms the right edge of PILGRIM'S PROGRESS, walk down this to the base. The first ascent took five hours car to car.

FA: Kurt Winkler and Joe Perez, February 9, 1980. On the first ascent, the two climbed the ice flow coming down off the rock overhang for 50 feet.

BASHO III 4 5.6

A thinly iced mixed climb on the far right end of the cliff band. At a series of rock overhangs, this flow ends distinctly 30 feet below a roof at an oak tree. The last pitch awaits completion. Cross the stream and walk directly up to a rock band below ice. Climb up snowy rocks to a 3 foot notched overhang, through this and left to a short rock step and trees above, then climb right to a two piton belay below the ice (5.6). The crux climbs the thinly iced rock above for 30 feet. Traverse left then up and exit right to a tree belay (long pitch, bring rock gear and short screws). Climb thickening bulges above an oak tree. Rappel down trees to the right of the climb.

FA: Ken Andrasko and Kurt Winkler, December 21, 1980. The first ascent took 5 hours and ended under a full moon.

East Royce Mountain

A.	RIGHTS OF SPRING	4	5.6	183
B.	CALIFORNIA KID	4-		183
C.	WHEN FRIGHT MEETS MIGHT	4+		183
D.	OPENING NIGHT JITTERS	4		184
E.	BALCONY SEAT	4		184
F.	EXIT STAGE LEFT	4+		184
G.	CURTAIN CALL	4		184
H.	EXIT STAGE RIGHT	3		184
I.	PROMPTER'S BOX	2		184
J.	THREE'S COMPANY	4		184
K.	PILGRIM'S PROGRESS	4		186

THE NORTH COUNTRY

This "land above the notches" abounds with ice. Spread out over a large geographic area are many climbing areas and individual routes that would shine bright if clustered down south. But lost in the north they have taken on an air of shrouded mystery, full of rumors and clues. It is probably safe to say that there are more routes still to be found than have been documented in this vast area. But then the lure of the north has always been rooted in the desire to explore.

Our research has turned up the following information. This is not an attempt to document every worthwhile route in The North Country. Rather we hope to remove some of the mystery, provide some basic information, and perhaps stimulate climbers to head north and see what they can find. Areas will be described approximately west to east.

BEAVER BROOK FALLS

BEAVER BROOK FALLS I 1-3
About three miles northeast of Colebrook N.H., on State Route 3 is BEAVER BROOK FALLS. A unique climb that is typically heavily mushroomed. Several variations are possible; descend off to the right.
FRA: Todd Swain and Matt Peer, solo, January 14, 1982.

MOUNT WINTHROP

MOUNT WINTHROP I 2-3
On Route 2, five miles east of its intersection with Route 16 in Gorham N.H., is an excellent practice area on the north side of Mt. Winthrop. Located directly opposite a public rest area, parking and access couldn't be more straightforward. The main feature is a 200 foot slab that is situated just off the highway, providing two pitches of low-angled ice. Descend to the left or rappel from trees. There are also some short, steeper flows off to the right.
FA: Unknown.

TUMBLEDOWN DICK MOUNTAIN

TUMBLEDOWN DICK MOUNTAIN I 2-4

Continue east on Route 2 past the junction with Route 113 (turning south leads to Evans Notch). Take the next road on the north and cross the Androscoggin River. Bear right and go a couple of miles to a pull-out under an obvious crag. This is the south side of Tumbledown Dick Mt., a popular rock climbing area for North Country residents, which has some interesting ice as well. Though there is no center-stage route here, pitches of up to grade 4 can be ferreted out of the crag if you don't mind doing a little exploring.

PINE MOUNTAIN

PINE MOUNTAIN I 3-4+

Take the road, locally called Flat Road, which leaves south from route 2 in the center of West Bethel, Maine, and follow it for about 2 miles until opposite an obvious iced face about a mile off the road on the west side of Pine Mt. Permission should be secured from landowners for parking and access to the cliff. There is a dirt road that leads to Trout Pond, just south of the cliff, that may make for the easiest approach. About a half a dozen flows will be found here ranging from 3 to 4+.

FA: Unknown. Jim Ewing may have explored here first.

RED ROCK MOUNTAIN

Located several miles east of Evans Notch, Red Rock Mountain. has several flows that will be of interest, especially for those with a flair for adventure considering that the approach may be the crux. There are two approaches, both of which will involve a four mile trip on skis or snowshoes. From the south take Route 5 north from Fryeburg, Maine, for about 12 miles passing through the small village of Lovell, and then continuing to the even smaller village of North Lovell. Turn left on West Lovell Road which leads around the northern tip of Kezar Lake (signs may still be visible for the defunct Evergreen Valley ski area). Go 1.8 miles then turn right on Hut Rd., just before the bridge over Great Brook. Continue for 1.5 miles to the trailhead for the Great Brook Trail. Follow that trail northwest for about 1.5 miles, passing the junction with the Miles Notch Trail. Shortly you will cross Great Brook. About a half a mile farther the trail crosses the brook again and a smaller brook comes in from the right at a culvert. This is Red Rock Brook which is now followed north, keeping to the left at any forks, for another 1.5 miles to an amphitheater on the south slopes of Red Rock Mt. The flows will be obvious.

From the north, follow the road, locally called Flat Road, which breaks south from Route 2 in West Bethel, Maine, opposite the West Bethel Post Office to a crossroads at 3.1 miles; take the road that runs west continueing straight ahead at another junction just past a small cemetery. How far you may be able to drive on these roads in the winter is entirely dependent on conditions.The Miles Notch Trail leaves at the end of the road and is followed for 2.4 miles to the junction with the Red Rock Trail which is followed an additional mile or so until near the summit of Red Rock Mt. The cliff at this point can best be accessed from the right (looking down) and may involve a rappel.

HOT LAVA II 4
Hot Lava is the most obvious of three or four flows on the face, the spectacular icefall reminiscent of Gully # 1 on Mt. Willard. The others have been climbed as well and are somewhat easier.There is also a 50 foot vertical curtain that will be passed on the southerly approach.
FA: Bob Parrott and Rob Adair, Winter, 1986.

DIXVILLE NOTCH

PARASOL GULLY II 2+
A beautiful route in a beautiful setting. Dixville Notch is located in northern N.H. northwest of the town of Errol on Route 26. At the very top of the notch on the south side is a very obvious 400 foot snow and ice gully. Strong updrafts in the notch often cause running water in the gully to freeze in horizontal sheets with thin fingers of ice at the edges. These "parasols," give the route its name.
FA: Jeff Pheasant, Steve Schneider, and Tad Pfeffer, Winter 1976.

GRAFTON NOTCH

A State Park about a half hour north of the town of Bethel, Maine (and about 1 1/2 hours from North Conway, N.H.) Grafton Notch contains a number of quality ice routes. From Bethel go north about six miles on Route 2 to the junction with Route 26 and take this north-west for about ten miles to reach the notch. Most of the climbing is on the south side of the notch in the vicinity of the Appalachian Trail parking lot. Short flows with a wide range of difficulties and easy approaches make the area attractive. Grafton Notch has been a favorite destination for climbers in southern and western Maine for decades and many have learned the basics playing on its friendly flows. Unfortunately the history of the region is sketchy, and accurate first ascent information is almost impossible to verify.

UNNAMED II 5

This is the longest, steepest route that one will see in the notch. It's about 1/2 mile south-east of the Appalachian Trail parking lot on the north side of the road. Two pitches of icicles and hanging columns call for a level head.
FRA: Pat Hackett and John Tremblay, Winter 1986/87.

A few hundred yards south of where the Appalachian Trail crosses the road is an excellent practice area on the south-west side of the road.. Slabs, bulges and a short, steep section all are easily top-roped.

For some added adventure a stream bed can be followed which offers many pitches of very easy snow and ice climbing. Higher up, the stream enters a cleft with moderate climbing and there are some pillars on the left which are about 40 feet high. In the woods farther left are additional bulges and short steep flows. The main stream bed can be followed for a considerable distance in this fashion, alternately walking and then scrambling, and parties have explored all the way up to Old Speck Mountain. There are also some huge slabs on Old Speck that have climbing similar to WILLEY'S SLIDE and have been used for decades as training routes.

Farther north, about a half mile past the Appalachian Trail, you will see ice up in the woods on the south-west side of the highway. This small amphitheater is a fine top roping area with many climbs in the grade 3-4 range. Park at the first logging road on the south-west side of the road and follow this into the woods for about fifty yards. (Do not block the logging road with your car.) The amphitheater trail now leaves the logging road on the left. The approach takes about a half hour. There are many short climbs here spread out in a semi-circle. A major feature is a strange twisting notch on the left side with a large icicle hanging down above. All routes are easily top-roped.

In addition to these areas there is also an obvious runnel of yellow ice that extends down the cliff on the left side of the cliff called the "Eyebrow."

YELLOW MUSTARD CUSTARD I 3+
Climbs the obvious yellow flow.
FRA: Matt Peer and Tim Retelle, late 1970's.

STACH I 2+
The neighboring and considerably easier flow.
FRA: Matt Peer and Tim Retelle, late 1970's.

MOUNT DIMMOCK

MOUNT DIMMOCK I 3
This small area is located in the village of Hanover, Maine, about 12 miles north of Bethel on Route 2. A road leads northwest from the center of town and very soon reaches Howard Pond. Before the pond, on the right side of the road, are two very obvious flows up in the woods on the south slope of Mt. Dimmock. Both are about two pitches long and in the grade 3 range with good, consistently thick ice.
FA: Unknown.

SQUAREDOCK MOUNTAIN

Travelling south on Route 5 from Bethel Maine, about a mile north of the junction with Route 35 in East Stoneham, a large rectangular cliff will be seen off to the west forming the southeast face of Squaredock Mountain. If coming from the south, pick up Rt. 5 in Fryeburg and go north about 20 miles to the junction with Rt. 35, then turn north on Rt. 5 for one mile. Park in the vicinity of a side road to the east and follow logging roads in towards the cliff. It is farther than it looks (allow at least an hour), but the reward is worth it. Just left of the cliff's center is a striking chimney system choked with ice.

BIG SCIENCE II 5
Follow the obvious chimney system for two pitches to the top. The crux is on the first pitch involving sustained climbing up icicles. Rock protection could

Bob Parrott and Rob Adair preparing for the second ascent of BIG SCIENCE, a classic back-woods route reminiscent of REPENTENCE.

Photo courtesy Bob Parrott

be helpful. This is a true backcountry classic that has been compared with the more urban REPENTENCE.
FA: Paul Boissonneault and Felix Modugno, Winter 1988.

BEAR MOUNTAIN

On Route 35 between Harrison and Waterford, next to the road and opposite Bear Pond, is a large broken cliff with a three pitch grade 3 chimney on the right as well as some practice flows to the left.
FA: Unknown.

MOUNT KINEO

MAINLINE III 5+

This is surely one of New England's most spectacular ice climbs, a thin, mushroomed ribbon that looks like it would be more at home in the Canadian Rockies. It may also be one of the hardest climbs just to get to. MAINLINE is located on the southwest face of Mt. Kineo, on Moosehead Lake, about 5 hours northeast of Mt. Washington. Road conditions can be treacherous as the last three hours or so are really in the outback. Self sufficiency is the name of the game for an ascent of MAINLINE, not only in terms of climbing the route itself, but also on the road-trip approach. Don't bother trying to call AAA, you probably couldn't find a phone anyway.

From the town of Greenville at the southern tip of Moosehead Lake head north along the western shore of the lake on Route 6/15. After about 20 miles you will come to the village of Rockwood. Moosehead Lake is very narrow at this point and Mt. Kineo and MAINLINE can clearly be seen across the lake to the north, about a mile away.

The climb is usually done in three pitches, the second being the crux, nearly a full pitch column of candled, mushroomed ice. It is possible in good conditions to avoid the very hardest section, but the climb will still be grade 5. Because the climb faces south, a prolonged cold spell is needed for it to form well, and even then the sun can do wierd things to the ice. Descend way around to the left (west).
FA: Clint Cummins and John Imbrie, around 1980.

UNNAMED III 4 5.6

Several hundred yards right of MAINLINE, on the east face of the cliff is another obvious route. This is a long mixed route.

FA: A bit sketchy, but Guy and Laura Waterman and Geoff Childs were known to have explored in the area. The first recorded ascent was by Kurt Winkler and Paul Boissonneault, Winter 1986.

Looking like it would be more at home in the Canadian Rockies, MAINLINE is perhaps the classic hard North Country route. Here Paul Boissonneault begins the first pitch. Photo by Ted Hammond

K A T A H D I N

Location:	Baxter State Park, Millinocket, ME. 6-8 hours from Boston.
Routes:	All grades, mixed, long.
Access:	12 mile ski, then 3 mile hike.
Descent:	Summer trails, easy gullies, exposed to weather.
Weather:	Summit, **severe!** see p. 18.
Equipment:	Many screws, rock gear, pins, 2 ropes, extra clothing.
Highlights:	New England's premier alpine area. *Long* gullies and buttresses, plus short, steep routes. *The Chimney, Waterfall, Walk on the Wild Side, Black Fly.*
Warning:	Pre-registration required. High avalanche danger.

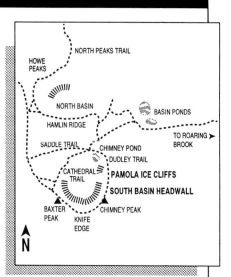

The Indians of the region named it "Katahdin, the Greatest Mountain"; thus, it need not be called "Mount Katahdin," just Katahdin. This giant rises to an altitude of 5,267 feet in Baxter State Park in northern Maine. Although the granite comprising Katahdin may be 300 million years old, the present height and shape of the mountain, with its famous Knife Edge and South and North Basins, is estimated to be a young 9,000 years old.

The first known winter ascent of Katahdin by a non-Indian was during the 1880's. It was a non-technical climb which followed various ridges to the top. In 1923, an AMC party climbed The Chimney, and qualified for the first technical winter ascent of Katahdin. Also, of note is the fact that part of that team succeeded in doing the first all-female ascent. Despite all of this activity so early, it wasn't until the 1970's that serious attempts on the East Face took place.

In February of 1971, George L. Smith led an impressive eleven-member

A rare look at early winter climbing in New England. Climbers from an AMC party struggle with the steep snow on the first ascent of THE CHIMNEY on Katahdin in 1923.
Photo by Comey

party in a Himalayan-style attempt on the East Face. Unfortunately, they failed when typically harsh winter conditions set in. A year later, John Porter's party succeeded in scaling the East Face. Although Porter modestly explained, "Our route is undoubtedly one of the easier possibilities," the GALLERY ROUTE was a major breakthrough and has had very few repeat ascents.

During the winter of 1972-73, Bob Proudman and his friends from the Pinkham Notch crew visited Katahdin twice. On the latter of the two trips, in March, they did seven routes, four of which were first winter ascents. Among these were THE DIAMOND and WATERFALL GULLY, both technically and psychologically demanding. Though their success was partly assured due to mild March weather, it wasnonetheless a very impressive tally.

The harsh winter of 1973-74 brought cold, high winds and little snowfall. Misha Kirk's party, whose members had just met for the first time for the climb, managed four winter ascents. With winds over 60 mph and temperatures dipping to -20 degrees at base camp, this was quite a feat considering that two of the party members had learned to climb just that summer. A month later, Bob Proudman returned. But this time disaster struck and Katahdin claimed its first winter climber. This accident is well documented in *Appalachia* and will always stand as a reminder of the seriousness of any Katahdin expedition.

In 1974-75, Rick Wilcox and John Bouchard visited the South Basin with a group of Chamonix guides. This group knocked off a few routes as part of their New England tour. Throughout the rest of the 1970's, other routes were completed by various well-known New England climbers.

The 1980's brought more climbers and more radical changes to Katahdin. Fast, alpine ascents became the standard. Geoff Heath's five hour solo ascent (Chimney Pond and back) of the CILLEY-BARBER ROUTE is an impressive example, as are explorations by climbers like Dave Getchell, Jr., Landon Fake, Kevin Slater, Kurt Winkler, Bob Baribeau and others.

Overshadowed by the larger peaks of New Hampshire's Presidential Range, Katahdin is easily underestimated. Though a thousand feet lower in elevation than Mt. Washington, Katahdin is much more rugged, and its harsh weather is notorious. Geologically younger, the mountain has sharper ridges, more jagged buttresses, and larger glacial cirques. In addition to its terrain, Katahdin's remote location and very limited facilities make rescues much more difficult. Self-sufficiency isn't just a good idea here, it is mandated, and all climbers must go through a complex registration procedure.

Perhaps more than any other alpine area in New England, slab avalanches are common on Katahdin. There have been several serious accidents, and knowledge in assessing avalanche danger is highly recommended. Routes to be particularly cautious of include: THE CHIMNEY WATERFALL GULLY, CILLEY-BARBER ROUTE, THE FUNNEL, THE DIAMOND, and THE BLACK GULLIES.

Every leader has the responsibility of assuring him or herself that the team is fit and properly experienced and has prepared for the intended venture. Bear in mind the variable weather and snow conditions. What might be a steep ice climb one year when snow is scarce, could be filled with snow to the point of being a fine ski run the next season.

Each party should contact the Baxter State Park for current regulations and information. Their address is Baxter State Park, 64 Balsam Drive, Millinocket, ME 04462, (207) 723-5149. No overnight activity is allowed in the park without a special winter use permit. The general regulations for any winter activity include: a request for a special winter use permit at least two weeks in advance, a leader and co-leader, with alternates, for each party, and a minimum of four people per party. In addition, for technical climbers, the party leader must file a statement of experience, and follow specific equipment, medical and itinerary restrictions. While there is a lot of paperwork involved with climbing at Katahdin, it is well worth the effort, and the regulations go a long way in preventing accidents.

Currently, one has to park several miles from the Togue Pond entrance, and hike or ski the twelve miles to Roring Brook Campground. You may have to undergo an equipment inspection at the park entrance. All parties planning to go to Chimney Pond will be required to spend their first night at Roaring Brook. It is an additional 3 1/2 miles to Chimney Pond. In addition to the bunkhouse which can accomodate up to 12 people, there is limited tent camping in the immediate area. The most up to date climbing information and notes on all the routes in the park will be found in a notebook at the rangers station at Chimney Pond.

From the bunkhouse at Chimney Pond, one has a commanding view of the East Face, with the Pamola Ice Cliffs on the left. The climbs on the main East Face can be reached by crossing the pond and continuing up the valley.

The climbs on the Pamola side involve short scrambles through deep drifts and prickly brush. Descents off the main part of the East Face are made down the Cathedral Trail (avalanche prone at timberline), the Dudley Trail or the Saddle Trail depending on your top-off point. The upper part of the Dudley Triail, the Knife Edge, is extremely exposed and is considered technical terrain in winter, while the Saddle Trail offers perhaps the least tiring descent. Descents from the top of the Pamola Ice Cliffs can be made from either end, (left easier) or in the middle where there is a gap between the Lower and Upper Ice Cliffs.

This beautiful area of New England offers some of the hardest, the longest, and particularly, the most remote climbs to be found in the region. Though regulations have been relaxed, they are still present, and every climber must consider whether Katahdin is indeed the place for them.

Note: The Baxter State Park Authority keeps a list of climbs, and for their rescue purposes, has numbered them from left to right, from the Cathedrals to the Pamola Ice Cliffs.

PAMOLA ICE CLIFFS

These dramatic ice cliffs, clearly seen across Chimney Pond on the southeast side of the South Basin, are home to Katahdin's steepest ice climbs. The climbs here are shorter than the big gully climbs, but make up for their small stature with unrelenting verticality. There are two parts to this section: an upper on the right (towards the Furies) and a lower one on the left (towards the Dudley Trail). The upper ice wall is broken up into four distinct routes, though many variations exist. The lower ice wall starts with MINI-PINNACLE #3 on the extreme left, and continues right ending at HANDS ACROSS THE WATER.

MINI-PINNACLE #3 I 2
This is a short gully found at the extreme left end of the rock band above Chimney Pond. One pitch up this fairly low angle gully. Descend off to the left. *FA: Unknown.*

MINI-PINNACLE #2 II 2
Found on the lower Pamola Ice Cliffs, this is the slightly larger gully and the second couloir in from the left. The first pitch is a moderate angled slab

trending from left to the right with a probable belay under the rock wall where the gully steepens. Move out left and up the bulge until the angle eases back. Descend off to the left, passing MINI-PINNACLE #2.
FA: Unknown.

ZORRO II 4
Count from the extreme left end (which is MINI-PINNACLE #1) and this will be the third climb in on your right on the lower Pamola Ice Cliffs. It takes a meandering line up through the center of the cliff. Work up through zig-zags of mixed snow and ice to any one of a number of potential belays. Continue up the gully climbing a steep bulge along the way. A descent can be made in either direction.
FA: A.J. LaFleur, Peter Cole, and John Bragg, mid 1970's.

STRANGE BREW II 3
Start just left of the HANDS ACROSS THE WATER, in a right-facing dihedral. Work your way to the base of the ice by traversing in on rock ledges from the left since the ice does not quite touch the ground. One very long pitch or two short ones will get you to the top. The crux lies in the first steep bulge as you enter the dihedral.
FA: Unknown.

HANDS ACROSS THE WATER II 4
Found at the right end of the lower section of the Pamola Ice Cliffs, or what would appear to be the closest ice flow to the pond. One or two pitches up the fairly steep and wide flow until it is possible to move off to the right and descend below the upper ice wall.
FA: John Bouchard, Rick Wilcox, and Claude Druyer, January, 1975.

FROST STREET II 5
This route is the farthest left of the major flows on the upper ice wall. A difficult route with scary climbing up a forty foot vertical crux section.
FA: John Imbrie and Dennis Drayna, December, 1979.

STAIRWAY TO HEAVEN II 4
Up a series of icicles from ledge to ledge. It is easier than it looks.
FA: Bob Proudman and Paul DiBello, January, 1974.

VARIATION: WHERE DO THE CHILDREN PLAY II 4+
Between STAIRWAY TO HEAVEN and WALK ON THE WILD SIDE

begin at a narrow and thin flow and then shallow gully to belay in semi-shattered alcove below a short, steep bulge. The second pitch climbs the bulge to easy ground and the top.
FRA: Jim Ewing and Rich Baker, January, 1984.

WALK ON THE WILD SIDE II 5

This classic route ascends the big, thck flow right of the previous route for two pitches. Slightly easier variations will be found on either side of the central line.
FA: Clint Cummins and Mike Lehner, February, 1975. Interesting historically is the ascent of a mixed route in the area in 1969 by Paul Ledoux and Al Rubin. This was most likely the first time that curved tools were used on Katahdin.

VARIATION: ICE-O-LATION II 4+

A short, two pitch route climbing steep columns on the left of SOUTH OF THE BORDER. After one long pitch, a short pitch gains the top.
FRA: Bob Baribeau, February 1983.

SOUTH OF THE BORDER II 4

This is the right-hand column found on the upper cliffs. Work up steep slabs to the base of the bulging wall. Then move up the ice above which is quite sustained, though just less than vertical at the steepest point. The second pitch is one full rope length.
FA: Tim Rouner and Peter Cole, January, 1974.

PAMOLA'S FURY LEFT III 3

About 130 yards right of the Pamola Ice Cliffs are two gullies. When viewed from the Cathedral Trail they appear similar, running parallel to each other as they rise more or less straight up to the summit of Pamola Peak. They are situated slightly to the left of a large slab that covers a fair amount of Pamola Peak. This left-hand gully is the more pronounced of the two and consists of several pitches of mixed snow and ice with intermediate sections of low-angle rock along the way. An avalanche runout usually marks the approach. At several points in the lower section it is possible to move right, climbing from one couloir to the next. Above, the ridge between the two climbs becomes more of a barrier.
FA: Bob Proudman, Mike Cohen and Doug George, February, 1974.

PAMOLA'S FURY RIGHT III 3

The right-hand couloir lies about 100 feet right of PAMOLA'S FURY LEFT

SOUTH OF THE BORDER, one of the Pamola Ice Cliffs' steepest lines.

Photo by Kevin Codraro

and is characterized by usually thin, icy slabs with an overlap about 200 feet. The direct route to the upper gully is poorly protected and most parties leave the gully earlier on the left heading for the Dudley Trail. In all expect about three pitches of climbing similar to, but steeper than WILLEY'S SLIDE.

The epic first ascent of this climb ended in tragedy with the team being benighted below the summit in horrible weather. Though a major rescue effort was quickly initiated , including a climbing team from from New Hampshire, it did not arrive in time to save Tom Keddy, who died at the bivuoac site. Paul DiBello, while surviving the ordeal, suffered crippling frostbite.
FA: Paul DiBello, Page Dinsmore, and Tom Keddy, February, 1974.

PAMOLA FOUR III 2+ 5.6
This is the skyline arete of Pamola that is clearly seen from Chimney Pond. Ascend moderate snow and ice slabs below the lower rock buttress of Pamola then traverse up and right to the base of the buttress. The route follows the center of the buttress for two pitches and then continues on the crest of the arete to the summit of Pamola.
FRA: Landon Fake and Kevin Slater, February, 1986.

SOUTH BASIN HEADWALL

A huge, dramatic glacial cirque, Katahdin's South basin is a fitting setting for New England's longest and most committing alpine routes. Climbs here vary from long snow gullies like the historic CHIMNEY, and hard water ice routes like the THE CILLEY- BARBER ROUTE, to difficult mixed climbs on the towering rock buttresses like the ARMADILLO. Many routes top out on the famous Knife Edge, a sharp ridge between the summits of Pamola and Baxter Peak. While spectacular, the climbs here share more than beauty and solitude. Fierce weather, frequent high avalanche danger, and a potentially long wait for rescue gives climbing here a serious air.

THE CHIMNEY II 2
The route is the large low-angled snow gully that separates Pamola Peak from The Knife Edge and the rest of the Katahdin massif. Very rarely is any ice found in the gully because the angle is so low that the snow depth becomes quite thick. Therefore, extreme care should be taken to avoid the couloir when the snow is new or when slab conditions are present. Wind slab avalanches of a few feet thick are not at all uncommon. The so-called 'first chockstone"

should be passed with care, since snow conditions in its vicinity are often dangerous. Descend via the Dudley Trail from the top of Pamola Peak, or glissade back down the gully if conditions are stable.

FA: Willard Helburn, Henry Chamberlain, Roger Holden, Owen Kennedy, Margaret Helburn, Jesse Dow, and Margaret Whipple, March, 1923.

VARIATION: STEEL MONKEY III 2 5.6

Begin in THE CHIMNEY and take the first narrow gully on the left. Climb for two pitches, passing a chockstone on the right (5.5). Four more pitches up another gully and onto a rock buttress will bring you back to THE CHIMNEY.

FA: Bob Baribeau and Kurt Winkler, February, 1989

LITTLE CHIMNEY (A.K.A. FALSE CHIMNEY) II 3

While a subsidiary couloir off the main chimney, this route takes an independent line for its entire length. The start of the route is found slightly right of THE CHIMNEY, and left of the first pitch of WATERFALL. You can either rejoin THE CHIMNEY by going left or take an independent line going right after the initial steep ice. The first ascent party bypassed some steep ice by rock climbing a chimney on the left which had a big rotten chockstone in the way. Near the top of the climb, the main gully fans out into three separate couloirs, each of which offer similar difficulties. Good rock belays will be found throughout the length of the route.

FA: Paul DiBello and Dana Jones, March, 1973.

WATERFALL GULLY IV 4+

Characterized by two impressive ice pillars at the beginning of the gully, this climb can be found several hundred yards left of THE CILLEY-BARBER ROUTE. From the base of the lower snow bowl, work your way left up to the base of the ice flows. Two pitches, the first one moderately steep and the second one an even more spectacular ribbon of ice, constitute the crux.

The remainder of the gully is predominently a snow climb as the route slowly turns a dog-leg right and joins the remaining ridge just east of The Cilley-Barber Route. You can also exit right (with one short rappel) after the first two pitches if you want a short climb or need to retreat.

FA: Mark Lawrence and Bob Proudman, March, 1973.

VARIATION: I 4

On the second pitch of WATERFALL GULLY, climb thin ice slabs on the left to a short pillar. Continue up and right joining the normal route.

FA: Landon Fake with assistance from Kevin Slater, March, 1987.

One of Katahdin's classic hard gullies, WATERFALL GULLY begins with some steep ice, and then eases off, giving many pitches of moderate terrain to the top.

Photo by Bob Parrott

VARIATION: WATERFALL GULLY EAST II 4

Same first two pitches as the former climb, except that after the crux, look for a diagonal snow gully coming in from the left. This is a long and committing route with some danger from avalanche.

FA: George Urioste, Mike Gilbert, Misha Kirk, and Joanne Selle, January, 1974.

WATERFALL BUTTRESS III 3+ 5.5

A large buttress divides the WATERFALL GULLY from THE CILLEY-BARBER ROUTE. This climb ascends an indistinct groove up the right side of the buttress. Approach up the first pitches of THE CILLEY-BARBER ROUTE, moving left after the first snowfiled. The buttress is climbed in about six pitches with delicate mixed climbing throughout.

FRA: Christine Baker and Landon Fake.

THE CILLEY-BARBER ROUTE IV 4

Left of the ARMADILLO, an ice flow descends all the way down to the lower snowfield. A long, aesthetic line, the CILLEY-BARBER is a classic. From the base of the bowl, work your way left up to the beginning of the first ice flow. The initial ice is low-angled, but becomes near vertical at the top. Many pitches of climbing lead to the top.

FA: Henry Barber and Dave Cilley, February, 1973.

VARIATION START: I 4+

An alternate first pitch climbs a rarely formed free-standing pillar.

FRA: Bob Baribeau and Kurt Winkler, 1Winter, 1988.

VARIATION FINISH: 4 5.7

A vertical flow at the top has been turned on the right via hard, mixed finish.

FA: Geoff Heath and partner, March, 1983

ARMADILLO IV 3+ 5.7

The most popular summer rock route at Katahdin becomes a very long and challenging mixed route in winther. Climb snow, ice and mixed ground to the western side of the Armadillo buttress. Climb the face to a chimney system for one pitch. Above swing left onto the exposed face and climb the to base of an obvious jamcrack. Climb the crack and then exit left to an arete which is followed for 3 to 4 pitches to the summit of South Peak.

FWA: Most likely by Michael Hartrich and Mark Whitton in February 1974.

Between the two obvious buttresses of The Armadillo and The Flatiron, an amphitheater is seen near the top of the ridge. This is the home of the following two routes. The easiest approach is up the lower stretches of THE CILLEY-BARBER ROUTE, then right as for THE DIAMOND, finally breaking up and left into the amphitheater. Neither route is very obvious. Many variations are possible, the hardest part of each route usually being near the top where cornices occasionally form.

BLACK GULLY EAST III 3
The left-hand line.
FA: Unknown.
BLACK GULLY WEST III 3
The right-hand line.
FA: Unknown.

THE DIAMOND IV 3+
Same start as for the GALLERY ROUTE, though this time one goes up the first gully to the right of The Flatiron. After many pitches of ice and snow in this gully, (usually thin and mixed) aim for a snowfield near the top that looks like a diamond. Proceed up the left edge of this snowfield and exit left.
FA: Bob Proudman and Paul DiBello, March, 1973.

GALLERY ROUTE III 3+ 5.6
Hiking up towards the left end of the lower cliffs, a hidden, slanting couloir runs directly up the left edge of the pyramid-shaped buttress which dominates the middle of the East Face. (An alternate start for this route, and THE DIAMOND begins up iced slabs of the the CILLEY-BARBER ROUTE, the most obvious break in the lower cliff band, and traverses right to a short, steep trough and continueing past the The Flatiron.) This brings one to a large snowfield above the lower cliffs. Continue up, traversing slightly right, until one is in the second gully to the right of The Flatiron. Continue up this gully for two pitches of sparsely protected 5.6 climbing (under normal winter conditions). Here, the angle eases back and the route continues up right in a slanting chimney to the final upper snow fields. Proceed five pitches up the couloir to the summit plateau. One rope-length south brings you to the Baxter summit.
FA: John Porter, Geoff Wood, Larry Nolin and Dave Isles, February, 1972.

CHAUVIN-COLE ROUTE III 3+
This route climbs the east face of Katahdin directly to the summit. Begin by ascending the large snowfield several hundred yards right of the start for

THE CILLEY-BARBER ROUTE. Above is a huge pyramid shaped buttress. Climb several pitches up a prominent snow gully to the right side of the buttress, then traverse up and left on mixed ground to an obvious shallow gully which is followed for five more pitches to the summit.
FA: Marc Chauvin and Peter Cole, Winter, 1982.

VARIATION START: II 3+ 5.6
Climbs the icy slabs of the buttress directly from the snowfield joining the upper trough after several mixed pitches.
FA: Bob Baribeau and John O'Brien, February, 1984.

PIGGY-WIGGY II 3
Farther right, this route was named for a stuffed animal which was the group's mascot. The first ascent party climbed two ice pitches up the lower slabs. After a precarious snowfield, which later avalanched, they came across a steep ice wall.   Three more pitches of ice will bring one to the upper snow bowl. Escape right towards THE FUNNEL or, as they did on the first ascent, left. At the top of the second snow bowl, bear left for two pitches of mixed climbing, and gain the ridge approximately 100 meters north of the summit.
FA: Misha Kirk, George Uriosite, Joanna Selle, and Mike Gilbert, January, 1974.

THE FUNNEL II 2+
The start and most of the route is the same as PIGGY-WIGGY, except that you exit right and then up an easy snow slope.
FA: Unknown.

DOUGAL'S DELIGHT II 2+
A tribute to the great Scottish ice climber. This climb starts on the shelf, just left of a bivy cave formed by a large rock. Start up the side ice flow and continue up for two pitches. The third pitch angles left onto a ridge. Some mixed climbing may be encountered here.
FA: Misha Kirk and Mike Gilbert, December, 1973.

GULLY #3 II 2
Between the Upper Cathedral Saddle and The Funnel, two gullies are found. GULLY #3 is the one closest to the Upper Cathedral Saddle. During most winters this is again an easy snow climb of several pitches. Head up towards the Upper Cathedral Saddle and angle left as the gully is entered.
FA: Unknown.

UPPER CATHEDRAL SADDLE (CATHEDRAL GULLY #2) II 1

In most winters this is an easy snow climb. A gully leads up to the Upper Cathedral Saddle .
FA: Unknown.

CATHEDRAL GULLY #1 II 1

Climb up the obvious line between the two rock cathedrals. Mixed climbing to deep snow conditions may exist on the route.
FA: Robert and Miriam Underhill, March,1923.

Note: these last three routes all can be used to descend toward Chimney Pond if weather conditions demand a fast descent.

NORTH BASIN

The climbing history of The North Basin is vague and short. Though Elbow Gully may have been climbed in the 1800's, most of the gullies have been explored in the 1970's and 1980's. The gullies in this area are usually steep snow routes rather than ice climbs and that may explain the relative lack of ice climbing activity.

Climbs in The North Basin can be made from Chimney Pond in a day, although it is a rather long one with a definite "alpine start." Take the summer trail to Blueberry Knoll. Just before reaching the knoll, take a left and bushwhack into The North Basin. Descents are made either by going left towards Hamlin Ridge (easier) or right passing Elbow Gully to the next gully north which can be downclimbed (or glissaded in good conditions) for 2,000 feet back to the base.

BLACK FLY IV 4/4+ 5.5

Left of Elbow Gully is a huge, 1000 ft. cliff. This classic route starts up the largest ice flow just left of a "nose-like" buttress on the left side of the cliff. The first ascent party encountered three pitches of steep ice followed by two pitches of steep snow. They then traversed left for one rope length and then up for three to four pitches of mixed ice and rock climbing.
FA: Dave Getchel, Jr. and Doug Carver, 1980's.

VARIATION FINISH: 5.6 mixed

At the top of the steep snow on BLACK FLY, instead of making the long

traverse to the left, head up and to the right following an obvious weakness for three more pitches to the top. A nice alpine climb.
FRA: Kurt Winkler and Bob Baribeau, Winter 1988.

HANTA YO IV 4 5.7

This impressive mixed route ascends the right flank of the huge wall between ELBOW GULLYand BLACK FLY. Begin at the base of ELBOW GULLY. Climb a short mixed pitch then traverse up the ELBOW GULLY ramp for another two pitches to a large red crack/chimney system on the left. Climb up this for 4 -5 pitches of 5.4 - 5.6 rock and then one pitch of steep, thin ice. A final pitch of rock (5.7) goes up and right to a headwall and the top.
FRA: Landon fake and Kevin Slater, February, 1987.

ELBOW GULLY III 1-2

Right of BLACK FLY and bordering the right edge of the large face is an obvious wandering gully that is narrow at the start and finishes up a wide basin. At the bottom of the gully is an obvious steep column. This is TUT"S THUMB. Scramble around this to the right to reach the start of the easy upper gully. Many pitches of mostly snow climbing lead to the top.
FA: Unknown.

TUT'S THUMB I 4+

Climbs very difficult ice as a direct start to ELBOW GULLY.
FRA: Andy Tuthill, Bob Parrott and Rob Adiar, February, 1986.

PAULA'S LAMENT II 3+

Above and to the right of the small tarn in the bottom of the basin is a this nice three pitch route that forms on the obvious slabs.
FRA: Bob Baribeau and Kurt Winkler, winter 1988.

Andy Tuthill breaking new (and steep!) ground on the first ascent of TUT"S THUMB, a
direct start to ELBOW GULLY in the North Basin.

Photo by Bob Parrott

Pamola Ice Cliffs

South Basin Headwall

Cathedrals — left

Cathedrals — right

North Basin — left

A.	VARIATION FINISH — BLACK FLY	mixed 5.6	210
B.	BLACK FLY	4-4+ 5.5	210

North Basin — Right

CAMDEN

Location:	Rt. 52, 2 miles northwest of Camden, ME.
Routes:	2-4+, gullies, thin slabs.
Access:	Park at base, 10 minute appproach.
Descent:	Scramble down through woods or rappel.
Weather:	*"Valley"*, proximity to ocean makes conditions sketchy, see pg. 18.
Equipment:	Standard ice rack, rock gear, thin ice protection.
Highlights:	Ocean view, many thin (exciting) routes.
Warning:	Many routes have very poor protection.

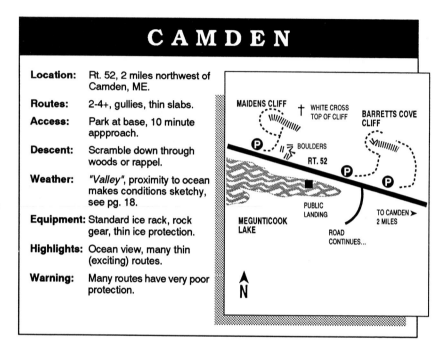

Skeptics might find it hard to believe that a little tourist town in mid-coast Maine hosts some of the scarier ice climbs in the East. Most Camden routes aren't overly steep, but many consist of sustained calf-burners on thin, low-angle ice — often above highly stimulating runouts. Think of Camden as ice climbing's equivalent to the Cannon and Whitehorse slabs.

The nearby ocean makes Camden winters somewhat erratic, though the long, cold nights of late December and January usually breed good ice. The thickest buildups occur after wet snowstorms followed by a couple of cold days. Since the cliffs face southwest, the sunny spells of February tend to wipe out the better routes. On the other hand, these sunny crags can be quite comfortable on those wicked days when it's -45° and blowing 100 up on Mt. Washington. And should you arrive to find the cliffs washed out by a dreary, cold rain...well, Camden also hosts several great restaurants and pubs.

From Portland, drive north on U.S. Route 1 about 1 1/2 hours; turn left onto Route 90 in Warren, then left (north) onto Rt. 1 again at Rockport (this saves about 1/2 hour); from Rockport, it's two miles to Camden. Total time: about two hours. Follow Rt. 1 thru Camden, and bear left onto Route 52 (also known as Mountain Street) just north of the village center. After about 2 miles, you'll crest a big hill and see the first of two major ice areas.

BARRETS COVE CLIFF

Park in a plowed turnoff directly below the crag, or at a lot (rarely plowed) about 100 yards farther on the cliff side of the road. Bushwhack 200 yards straight up to the base, or follow the faint summer climber's trail just left of the talus.

The cliff averages about 200 feet high, with a wide ledge (Broadway) at half height. Most routes involve two or three pitches, often with significant sections of mixed terrain. Start climbs here early; it's not unusual for certain routes to be in fine shape in the morning and gone by mid-afternoon.

The moderate climbs follow lower-angle chimneys and flows where protection is generally adequate with screws (bring some short ones) and a rack of rock gear. The harder lines launch out onto alarmingly thin smears up 70-degree faces with spotty or non-existent pro; bring sharp hooking tools, swing 'em gently, and don't look down! Bolts and fixed gear are rare here, though tied-off screws, Spectres (driveable, pick-shaped hooks for protection on thin ice), TCUs, Friends and small wires help lend some sense of security.

There are several descent options from the top of the cliff. Sketchy trails can be followed down either side, to the left (north) dropping into a creek bed that leads back to the base, or to the right (south) angling away from the cliff into open woods that will lead back to the road. (don't cut back toward the base until you are almost to the road, unless you enjoy downclimbing vertical moss bulges.) The other option is to rappel the cliff with two ropes from trees above CHARLOTTE'S CRACK, once to a 3 bolt anchor on Broadway, and then again to the ground. Route descriptions run left to right.

ARIZONA HIGHWAYS I 3+ to 4
Start near the cliff's far left margin at a thin smear leading to a gully. The obvious hanging columns above (4) can be bypassed up ramps to the right. *FA: Geoff Heath, Pete McCartney, 1977.*

SOLSTICE WALL I 4+ 5.8
A steely line tiptoeing up a rarely-formed smear above the right end of a long, low roof. Cruise the moderate gully, pass the start of Broadway ledge,

and belay in a chimney about 30' higher. Take a deep breath, traverse a brushy crack left (last pro), and finesse up the thinly iced face above. Rock gear is crucial, as is an early start.

FA: Geoff Heath and Dave Getchell, Sr., Winter Solstice, 1981.

CHARLOTTE'S CRACK 1 5.7

This is the summer trade route up a diagonal crack above BIG CHIMNEY. It rarely ices up, and in winter serves mainly as a quick rappel route. Rap with two ropes from trees to a 3-bolt anchor on Broadway, then another two-rope rap to ground.

PHARAOH'S BEARD I 3+

A fine, fun line on the upper wall. From Broadway, follow the distinctive triangular flow marked by a pine jutting horizontally at the top. Usually thick enough to take ice screws.

FA: Dave Getchell, Sr., Geoff Heath and Pete McCartney, 1977.

BIG CHIMNEY I 2-3

Just right of a huge block at the base, this deep, vegetated cleft ices up in good snow years, giving easy access to Broadway. Other years, it's desperately thin and not recommended.

FA: George Smith, 1960s .

SKYE CRACK I 3+ 5.4

About 30' left of the main HEATHROW gully, an ice ribbon leads up to a juniper and a (hopefully) ice-choked offwidth crack, then up mixed ground to trees on Broadway (160'). Typically the first protection comes 50-60 feet up; after that, use rock gear to 3".

FA: Geoff Heath and Dave Getchell, Sr., 1978 .

HEATHROW II 3

The huge central gully offers the cliff's most reliable ice. The first 80' are rarely protectable, but at least they're low-angled. If in doubt, follow the left-hand lower flow into an alcove, then slightly right up a short bulge (good wires) to a ramp and fixed pin; step right to the ledge, and belay atop the projecting block (165', can be split). From Broadway, bash up blue ice straight to the trees (100'); going right and up the gully leads to shaky mixed ground. A fine narrow flow sometimes forms left of a notch at the top.

FA: Ken Clark, early 70s.

Geoff Heath on an early ascent of PHAROAH'S BEARD on Barrett's Cove Cliff. Note all the great pro!

Photo by Dave Getchell, Sr.

CLOTHESLINE I 3-4

An ice-hose leads up a squeeze chimney just left of HEATHROW's top pitch. It's nice when thick, but very scary when thin. Take screws, small wires, and mid-size camming units.

FA: Dave Getchell, Jr., and Pete McCartney, 1977.

DESPERADO I 4+

This outlandish smear clings very occasionally to the steep slab right of HEATHROW. Rarely more than an inch or two thick, the ribbon ends in a corner 80' up; don't count on any pro before that. Belay there, calm down, then finish up HEATHROW.

FA: Geoff Heath and Michael Opuda, 1982.

JOE'S ROUTE I 2

An enjoyable, non-demanding mixed climb. Follow the line of least resistance up the gully right of HEATHROW, then up low-angle ramps leading right to a huge pine. 2-3 pitches.

FA: Pete McCartney and Dave Getchell, Sr., 1977.

CONTINENTAL ICE SHEET II 3+ 5.6

High on the right wall, a big cascade marks the airiest, most sustained line on the cliff—and it even has pro if the ice is good. Start up JOE'S ROUTE and belay in one of two left-facing corners below the main flow. Launch up the columns onto the exposed ice sheet above (optional belay in a cleft), then scramble up left on mixed ground (165').

FA: Geoff Heath, Pete McCartney, Dave Getchell, Sr., 1979.

BIG CITY WOMAN I 3 5.7

This obvious ice tongue right of CONTINENTAL ICE SHEET stops short of the top, so rock-climb left into a flared chimney. Wild, but well protected with a few pitons.

FA: Geoff Heath and Dave Getchell, Jr., 1982.

TANGLED UP IN BLUE II 3+/4 5.7

A committing last pitch, but worth the wait for it to appear. Start on the cliff's lower tier below JOE'S ROUTE, up the middle flow to a big pine. Ramps and a chimney lead to a belay ledge. The rarely formed crux pitch goes between CONTINENTAL and BIG CITY WOMAN, up thin cracks and dicey ice. Bring small wires and big confidence.

FA: Dave Getchell, Jr., and Geoff Heath, 1983.

Dave Getchell, Jr. on the crux ice hose of CLOTHESLINE, Barrett's Cove Cliff.
Photo by Dave Getchell, Sr.

TRITIUM WITCH I 2/3

This moderate flow on the right of the upper wall gives a good finish to JOE'S ROUTE, and offers a sane alternative if TANGLED UP IN BLUE or BIG CITY WOMAN have fallen off.
FA: Dave Getchell, Jr., and Geoff Heath, 1979.

To the right and down from HEATHROW and below JOE'S ROUTE, a broken-up area hosts several nice top-rope flows (scramble off right) and direct starts to JOE'S ROUTE and TANGLED UP IN BLUE. From left to right:

WATERFALL 3+

The wide, bulgy flow on the left.
FA: Unknown.

TANGLED UP IN BLUE DIRECT START 3+

Up steeper stuff in the middle.
FA: Unknown.

JOE'S DIRECT 2+

Go up a short bulge and snow ramp to alcove, then a pitch up the left-facing corner/gully to join JOE'S ROUTE.

MAIDEN CLIFF

High on the western flank of Mt. Megunticook, a mile or so past Barrett's Cove Cliff, a tall white cross marks where a little girl fell to her death in the 1880s. Below the memorial, deep gullies hide several fine ice lines. The routes are hard to see from Route 52 but show up better from out on the frozen lake. Park where the talus comes close to the road, just before a group of cottages along the lakeshore. There is usually a plowed turnout on the cliff side of Route 52. Bushwhack for two hundred yards straight up through the talus. The cliffs here are fairly broken up, with lots of trees, but you can find a number of 2-3 pitch routes in a good year. The flows are steeper than Barrett's, more on the order of Frankenstein-style pillars and gullies. Descend by rappel from trees, or scramble down a narrow gully off left.

DOUBLE CLUTCH I 4

This is the left-hand ice tower just right of the descent gully, with an

overhanging curtain at half height. An undercling past the curtain explains the name.
FA: Dave Getchell Jr., and Pete McCartney, 1982.

KISS OF THE SPIDER WOMAN I 4
A free-standing pillar forms infrequently to the right of DOUBLE CLUTCH. Most years, you have to aid past the rock overhang to reach the steep ice gully above (5.8 A1).
FA: Gerry Cinnamon and partner, 1985.

PETE'S PUZZLE I 3 5.7
Right of SPIDER WOMAN, follow thin ice and mixed ground into a narrow alcove; puzzle out of the slot (fixed peg) and onto a verglassy slab. Finish at will up gullies and flows above (300 feet).
FA: Dave Getchell, Sr., and Pete McCartney, 1980 .

BLUE VEIN I 4 5.8
Approach via a steep gully marked by a pine a few hundred yards south along the road. A tight chimney on the right provides what some call Camden's finest ice climb. Technical groveling to reach a cool ice hose deep in the crack usually forms the crux; thinly iced overhangs above cap off the experience.
FA: Geoff Heath and Dave Getchell, Sr., 1980.

Barretts Cove Cliff

Maidens cliff

ACADIA NATIONAL PARK

Famous for its clean granite and unique seaside setting, Acadia is also home to some ice climbing. Typically mild winters make things a little hit-or-miss but in a normal winter the following routes usually come into shape.

Another forty-five minutes or so up the coast on Route 1 from Camden turn south in Ellsworth and drive about 20 miles to the park. Most of the park's Loop Road is open in the winter and camping is available at Blackwoods Campgound.

CEDAR CHEST I 3

JORDAN CLIFF DIRECT I 4

These two routes are both located on the far side of Jordan Pond, right off the Loop Road. Access is across the pond if well frozen or around the ends. Both climbs are two to three pitches.

OTTER CLIFF I 4+

Renowned as a rock climbing area for its seacliff atmoosphere, Otter Cliff occasionally sports a unique ice climb as well. To the left of the prominent Sea Stack by a couple of hundred feet or so an ice curtain sometimes forms giving fifty feet of vertical climbing on frozen sea-spray. Usually top-roped.
FA: Unknown.

In addition to these routes, other short climbs will be found along Sargent Drive next to Somes Sound, at the Hull's Cove quarry, and along the loop road on the south face of Champlain.

INDEX BY AREA BY DIFFICULTY

NOTE: Routes have not been ranked in order of difficulty within the sub-grades. The first route listed as a 3+ is not neccessarily easier than the last route listed as a 3+. Routes with rock climbing grades only should be considered mixed routes under typical conditions.

Area/Route	Rating		Page
	Ice	Rock	
Cannon Cliff continued			
LA DEEPFREEZE	2-3	—	72
CANNONADE	2-3	5.4	77
LILA	4+	A2	75
QUARTET ICE HOSE	4+	5.8 A2	77
THE BLACK DIKE	5-	—	73
VARIATION — HASSIG'S DIRECT	5	—	75
FAFNIR	5	—	75
OMEGA	5+	—	72
The Eaglet			
SHORT TRICK	3	—	80
TRUMP CARD	3	—	80
GARCIA-VEGA	4	—	80
ACE OF SPADES	4	—	81
OVERBID	4+	—	80
Mount Garfield			
UNNAMED	4	—	81
SICK PUP	4+	—	81
POSTHOLE ALFONSO	4+	—	81
MAD DOG	5	—	81
THE BIG ONE	5	—	81
BAKER RIVER VALLEY			
Newfound Lake			
BLOODLINE	3	—	83
SLIM JIM	3+/4	5.6	83
DUOFOLD	4	—	83
PIKE LINE	4	—	83
RED HEADWALL	5	—	83
Rattlesnake Mountain			
CENTERFOLD	3	—	84
GRADE 3	3	—	84
SCOTTISH COWBOY	3	—	84
THE CAVE ROUTE	3	—	86
MANDIBLE	3+	—	85
DUSTBOWL	3+	5.6	89
THE MEADOW	3-5	—	84
DANDRUFF	4-	—	86
ICE-OLATOR	4	—	88
K-9	4	—	88
LEARNING DISABILITIES	4	—	85
POLAR PILE	4	—	88
SELSUN BLUE	4	—	86
SOFFIT BREATH	4	—	89
VENEER	4	—	85
PRESTOR JOHN	4	—	89
PRIVATE EYE	4+	—	85

ANTORCR

Area/Route	Rating Ice	Rock	Page
Rattlesnake Mountain continued			
HULA HOOP	4+	5.7	88
JOHN'S PILLAR	5-	—	89
SASQUATCH	5-	—	89
FANGMANSHIP	5	—	88
JAWS PILLAR	5	—	85
FRANKY LEE	5	—	85
PRESTOR PILLAR	5	—	89
BARBADOS	5	—	84
GALAPAGOS	5	—	84
PSORIASIS	5	—	86
THE GEOGRAPHIC FACTOR	5	—	89
ARTIFICIAL INTELLIGENCE	5	5.8	86
OLIVARIAN NOTCH			
Owl's Head Cliff			
SNAKE ATTACK	4	—	90
THE FEAR OF LIVING DANGEROUSLY	4	—	90
KINSMAN NOTCH			
KILARNEY	1-2	—	91
LEPRECHAUN'S LAMENT	2-3+	—	91
BLARNEY STONE	3	—	91
POT O' GOLD	4	—	91
LUCK O' THE IRISH	4+	—	91
KANCAMAGUS HIGHWAY			
Black Mountain			
LONG WAY HOME	2-3	—	92
Mount Osceola			
ON THE DROOL OF THE BEAST	5-	—	93
Mount Huntington			
SHEER ELEGANCE	4+	5.6	93
Mount Hedgehog			
CHOCKSTONE CHIMLEY	3	5.6	93
Pitcher Falls			
PITCHER FALLS	3-4+	—	94
Crack in the Woods Cliff			
BOSSANOVA	3	—	94
ANGELS DON'T SHATTER	3	—	95
COLUMN IN THE WOODS	4	—	94
Rainbow Slabs			
RAINBOW SLABS	2-3+	—	95

Area/Route	Rating		Page
	Ice	*Rock*	
Frankenstein Cliff continued			
DRACULA	4+	—	142
FANG	4+	—	132
THE SPACEMAN	4+	—	134
THE SWORD AND THE STONE	4+	—	132
THE WRATH OF THE VALKYRIE	4+	A3	132
HOBBIT COULOIR	4+	—	136
DRACULA — RIGHT-HAND SIDE	4-5	—	144
SLIM PICKENS	5-	—	135
ANGEL CAKE	5-	—	146
BRAGG/PHEASANT	5	—	134
DROPLINE	5	—	141
LAST EXIT	5	—	142
WELCOME TO THE MACHINE	5	—	142
WIDOW'S WALK	5	—	139
THE BROWN RECLUSE	5	—	139
WITHOUT REASON	5+	—	144
Lost Helmet Crag			
THE SNUGCICLE	2-3	—	146
ROBOT LOGIC	3+	—	147
TAP TAP CRASH	3+	—	147
EXTENSOR	4+	—	147
Mount Webster			
HORSESHOE GULLY	1-2	—	154
NORTH SLABS	1-2	—	155
SHOESTRING GULLY	2-3	5.5 finish	154
LANDSLIDE GULLY	2-3	—	154
CENTRAL COULOIR	2-3+	—	154
THE PILGRIMAGE	3	—	156
FOOL'S PARADISE	3	—	155
HALF BREED	3	5.2	155
GREEN CHASM	3	5.6	155
HEART PALACE	4-	—	155
Willey's Slide			
WILLEY'S SLIDE	2	—	156
STREAMLINE	2	—	156
FLAT FOOT FLOOGIE	2+	—	157
CANDLEPIN	4	—	157
Mount Willard			
CINEMA GULLY	2	—	160
CAULIFLOWER GULLY	2-3	—	161
HITCHCOCK GULLY	2-3	—	161
THE CLEFT	2-3	—	161
FREEZE FRAME	3	5.7	160
LONG DISTANCE LOVE	3	—	162

Area/Route	Rating		Page
	Ice	Rock	
Pamola Ice Cliffs continued			
ICE-O-LATION — VARIATION	4+	—	202
FROST STREET	5	—	201
WALK ON THE WILD SIDE	5	—	202
South Basin Headwall			
CATHEDRAL GULLY #1	1	—	210
UPPER CATHEDRAL SADDLE (GULLY#2)	1	—	210
GULLY #3	2	—	209
THE CHIMNEY	2	—	204
STEEL MONKEY — VARIATION	2	5.6	205
DOUGAL'S DELIGHT	2+	—	209
THE FUNNEL	2+	—	209
PAMOLA FOUR	2+	5.6	204
BLACK GULLY — EAST	3	—	208
BLACK GULLY — WEST	3	—	208
LITTLE CHIMNEY (A.K.A. FALSE CHIMNEY)	3	—	205
PIGGY-WIGGY	3	—	209
CHAUVIN-COLE ROUTE	3+	—	208
THE DIAMOND	3+	—	208
WATERFALL BUTTRESS	3+	5.5	207
VARIATION START (CHAUVIN-COLE ROUTE)	3+	5.6	209
GALLERY ROUTE	3+	5.6	208
ARMADILLO	3+	5.7	207
WATERFALL GULLY EAST — VARIATION	4	—	207
VARIATION (WATERFALL)	4	—	205
THE CILLEY-BARBER ROUTE	4	—	207
VARIATION FINISH (CILLEY-BARBER ROUTE)	4	5.7	207
VARIATION START (CILLEY-BARBER ROUTE)	4+	—	207
WATERFALL GULLY	4+	—	205
North Basin			
VARIATION FINISH (BLACK FLY)	—	5.6	210
ELBOW GULLY	1-2	—	211
PAULA'S LAMENT	3+	—	211
BLACK FLY	4-4+	5.5	210
HANTA YO	4	5.7	211
TUT'S THUMB	5	—	211
CAMDEN			
Barretts Cove Cliff			
CHARLOTTE'S CRACK	—	5.7	220
JOE'S ROUTE	2	—	222
JOE'S DIRECT	2+	—	224
BIG CHIMNEY	2-3	—	220
TRITIUM WITCH	2-3	—	223
HEATHROW	3	—	220
BIG CITY WOMAN	3	5.7	222
CLOTHESLINE	3-4	—	222

INDEX BY ROUTE

Area/Route	Rating		Page
	Ice	*Rock*	
JOB'S PILLAR	4	—	69
JOB'S POND	—	—	69
JOE'S DIRECT	2+	—	224
JOE'S ROUTE	2	—	222
JOHN'S PILLAR	5-	—	89
JORDAN CLIFF DIRECT	4	—	228
KANCAMAGUS HIGHWAY	—	—	92
KATAHDIN	—	—	196
KATAHDIN — NORTH BASIN	—	—	210
KATAHDIN — SOUTH BASIN	—	—	204
KILARNEY	1-2	—	91
KING RAVINE	—	—	177
KING RAVINE HEADWALL	1-2	—	177
KINSMAN NOTCH	—	—	90
KISS OF THE SPIDER WOMAN	4	—	225
K-9	4	—	88
LABYRINTH WALL, THE (all free 5.11+)	—	5.7 A4	78
LA DEEPFREZE	2-3	—	72
LAKEVIEW	2	5.5	79
LAKE WILLOUGHBY	—	—	54
LAMINATE, THE	5	—	122
LANDSLIDE GULLY	2-3	—	154
LAST EXIT	5	—	142
LAST GENTLEMAN, THE	5	—	58
LEARNING DISABILITIES	4	—	85
LEDGE APPROACH — VARIATION	4	—	57
LEFT FLOW	4	—	68
LEFT WALL OF CENTRAL GULLY	2	—	174
LEPRECHAUN'S LAMENT	2-3+	—	91
LILA	4+	A2	75
LITTLE CHIMNEY (A.K.A. FALSE CHIMNEY)	3	—	205
LONG DISTANCE LOVE	3	—	162
LONG WAY HOME	2-3	—	92
LOST HELMET CRAG	—	—	146
LOST IN THE FOREST	2-3	—	140
LUCK O' THE IRISH	4+	—	91
LUNA GLACE	3+	—	121
MAD DOG	5	—	81
MADISON GULF	—	—	176
MAIDEN CLIFF	—	—	224
MAINLINE	5+	—	194
MAIN FLOW	3	—	68
MANDIBLE	3+	—	85
MEADOW, THE	3-5	—	84
MEAN MISS TREATER	4	–	140
MELLOW YELLOW	3	—	166
MINDBENDER	5+	—	55
MINES OF MORIAH	—	5.7 A2	110
MINI-PINNACLE #2	2	—	200
MINI-PINNACLE #3	2	—	200
MIS-GUIDED	3	–	123
MOAT MOUNTAIN ICE FALL	2	—	99

ABOUT THE AUTHOR

Photo credit: Celia Davis

Rick Wilcox

Rick has been climbing since 1964. In 1969 he began working for Eastern Mountain Sports as store manager and climbing instructor in North Conway, NH. He became director of the EMS Climbing School in 1974 and ran it until 1979 when he left EMS to take over International Mountain Equipment, Inc. Since 1977, Rick has been president of the Mountain Rescue Service.

Throughout twenty-eight years of mountaineering and climbing, Rick has climbed in many of the world's major mountain ranges with over twenty expeditions to the Andes, Alaska, and the Himalalaya, including a successful ascent of Mount Everest in 1991.

ABOUT THE EDITOR

S. Peter Lewis

Peter began climbing in 1977, and has worked part-time as a climbing guide since 1982. He began his journalism career in 1983 working as a climbing photographer and writer for outdoor magazines. In 1988 he moved to newspaper photojournalism and writing and has since then received numerous awards for his work including being chosen N.H. Press Association Photographer of the Year two years running.

Peter's background in writing and photography have led him into the field of editorial design where he now combines his talents on a wide range of projects.

Peter lives in Fryeburg, Maine with his wife Karen and their two children Jeremiah and Amanda.